Bridal Showers

BY

BEVERLY CLARK

Special Touches and Unique Ideas
for Throwing a Fabulous Shower

WILSHIRE PUBLICATIONS

To my husband, for his encouragement, support, and understanding.

Published by Wilshire Publications
Beverly Clark Collection

Distributed by:
Publishers Group West, Emeryville, CA

Beverly Clark Collection
1120 Mark Avenue
Carpinteria, CA 93013
(800) 888-6866

Publisher's Cataloging-in-Publication
(Provided by Quality Books, Inc.)

Clark, Beverly.
    Bridal showers : special touches and unique
ideas for throwing a fabulous shower / Beverly
Clark. — 1st ed.
        p. cm.
        Includes index.
        ISBN 0-934081-18-2

    1. Showers (Parties)   2. Menus.   I. Title

GV1472.7S5SC57 2000   783.2
                                              QBI99-1734

Edited by: Gail Kearns, Robin LaFevers, Penelope C. Paine
Cover Design: Victoria Torf Fulton
Book Layout and Typography: Cirrus Design

CONTENTS

INTRODUCTION

WHEN HOSTING A SHOWER for a close friend or relative, whether it be your first time or your fiftieth, you will want it to be as special as the person you're giving it for. With a little additional thought and attention to detail, you can turn what might otherwise be just another ordinary shower into a smashing success. Surprise your guests with imaginative decorations, challenging games, and delightful party favors.

There is more to creating a memorable event than tasty food and fabulous decorations. A successful party also depends on your ability to make your guests feel completely at ease. This is accomplished by a hostess who is prepared and organized. Use the tips, checklists, and worksheets provided to help you prevent oversights and frantic last-minute rushing.

Choose from a number of shower themes, or combine portions of a few and design a shower that is uniquely yours. This book is intended to give you creative ideas that will spark your imagination so you can assemble an affair that will reflect your taste and that of the future bride and groom.

1

HOSTING A BRIDAL SHOWER

The History of a Cherished Tradition

THE FIRST BRIDAL SHOWER was said to have taken place in Holland when a young girl fell in love with a poor but generous miller. Over the years the miller had given away all his possessions to those needier than himself so that when the time came to wed he had nothing left to offer his prospective bride.

Furious with his daughter's choice of suitors, her father forbade the marriage and refused the young pair the customary dowry, which was necessary to establish a household. Without it the pair had little hope of being able to begin a life together. It was then that the community came to the couple's rescue. Out of appreciation for the miller's benevolence, his friends banded together and literally "showered" the young girl with all the items necessary to set up a house. It was the beginning of a long marriage and a beautiful tradition.

Who Hosts a Shower

A vestige of the old-fashioned dowry each bride received from her family, the bridal shower has remained a special gift given the bride by her "family of friends." The party is customarily hosted by the maid of honor or the bridesmaids. It may also be held by a relative, close friend, or even a co-worker of either the bride-to-be or her mother. Formerly, strict rules of etiquette precluded the mother or sister of the bride from serving as hostess since presents are expected. More recently, however, this rule has been relaxed and it has become not only acceptable but also quite customary for the immediate family to host the shower. Even if immediate family members do not host the event itself, they may wish to be included by either helping to defray some of the costs involved or by offering their home as a location for the party. If the ladies in the bridal party are jointly hosting the shower, the responsibilities should be evenly divided. One individual, usually the maid of honor or the one whose home is used, acts as the shower coordinator.

It is not necessary to be invited to the wedding in order to host a shower. This is particularly true if you are a co-worker or business associate who wants to celebrate this special event but are not close enough friends with the bride to receive an invitation to her wedding.

Hosting a Shower for the Encore Bride

Since the original purpose of a wedding shower was to help the bride set up her first household, showers generally were not held for the bride who was remarrying. Today, the original intent of the event has generally been disregarded, with showers for the encore bride being held in the spirit of a prenuptial party for the pair. Although formality and style may vary, these showers are usually simpler. In keeping with the tone of a second marriage ceremony, the shower is smaller with less elaborate decorations. In addition, gifts tend to be of a more personal nature rather than items for the household.

Who's Invited

Since bridal showers tend to be more intimate occasions than weddings, usually only the closest of friends and relatives are invited. The exception is the party given by an office staff, sorority, or club. Formerly, bridal showers were women-only afternoon gatherings which tended to adhere to the same format. Now, changing times have given this affair an updated look with the only limit being your imagination. As the average age of bridal couples has increased, so has the participation of men in all aspects of the wedding and its accompanying festivities. No longer strictly for women, bridal showers now place a new emphasis on couples. Couples showers, which honor both the bride and groom, are increasingly in demand with both evening parties and barbecues lending themselves nicely to this now popular option.

If there will be two or more showers held, make sure that the guest list is not redundant. With the exception of the immediate family, the same guest should be invited to only one or two parties at the most. To avoid straining the pocketbooks of those attending two showers, you may want to emphasize to these prospective guests that their presence at the second shower is enough of a gift. For those who might still feel uncomfortable coming "empty-handed," a few fresh flowers from the garden would be a welcomed addition to the festive table. If you know the other people who are also planning to host a shower, you may want to get in touch with them about the possibility of combining parties and cohosting one large party in place of several smaller ones. It's a great way to ease some of the burden placed on the hostess and avoid duplication of guest lists.

Keeping in mind both your budget and the number of guests your prospective location will comfortably accommodate, tentatively establish the number you wish to invite. Then consult with the bride regarding the guest list. Most showers have between 10 and 30 guests with couples parties having as many as 40 celebrants. If you are hosting a surprise shower, contact the bride's mother and/or her fiancé to get the wedding guest list. Also ask for the names and addresses of special friends and relatives who should be included.

Usually those invited to the shower will also be attending the wedding. There are exceptions, however, such as in the case of the office or club-sponsored shower. Also, small "family-only" or out-of-town ceremonies will naturally limit the number of shower guests who will also be present at the nuptials.

The Invitation

Unless the invitations are to be extended informally by telephone, the hostess should mail them out no later than three to four weeks before the shower. Handwritten invitations are generally preferred except in the case of a small shower with only very close friends or an informal, last-minute get together.

The wide variety of preprinted invitations currently available, as well as the freedom to use your own creative ideas, can insure that your invitation reflects and reinforces the style or theme of your special event. In most cases, the pertinent information is handwritten. Try a touch of calligraphy to add creative flair. For a large, elegant shower, such as a couples cocktail party or formal dinner, you may prefer to have the entire invitation custom printed.

Today, with the easy-to-use desktop publishing software, "doing it yourself" deserves consideration. Special pre-designed papers and cards can be purchased at copy centers and office supply stores for computer-generated invitations. Scanners and digital cameras allow for customized and personalized cards and announcements. Your invitation can be created on your home computer and, saved to disk, taken to your local copy shop and printed in color on card stock. As your invitations are priced per piece, you need only to print and pay for what you need.

Look for blank greeting cards at your local stationery store or bookstore. You may find something suitable that reflects your shower theme.

What to Include

Whether you use a preprinted invitation, a computer-generated one, or another of your own design, be sure to include the following:

- ~ Name of the host or hostess. When the entire bridal party is hosting the shower, you may either list the individual names or simply state "given by the bridal party."
- ~ Name of the person the shower is honoring.

~ The date and time of day.

~ The address.

~ Travel directions. A must for those not familiar with the location, you should be sure to include a separate piece of paper with a small map or clear directions. Don't forget to include the telephone number of the house or facility where the party will take place, just in case someone gets lost on the way.

~ RSVP with a telephone number. To ensure more responses, you may opt to include a deadline for replies.

Additional Information

You may want to include any or all of the following somewhere on your invitation:

~ The shower theme (kitchen, entertainment, around-the-world, etc.)

~ Special requirements of your particular shower. In the case of an Around-the-clock shower, for example, you need to designate the specific time of day each guest has been assigned and what this means (See Shower Themes.) If you are having a recipe shower, don't forget to include a recipe card with instructions on how you want it to be filled out. In the case of a surprise shower, be sure to emphasize it on the invitation.

Practical information to help your guests in selecting a gift.

~ Guests should know exactly which colors and accessories the bride has selected for her decor, as well as where she is registered.

~ In the case of a lingerie shower, don't forget to include her size!

~ Searching for the perfect present can quickly become a burden to those with busy schedules. Do your guests a favor by encouraging the bride to register at a local store which carries items appropriate for your shower. It reduces the guesswork by clearly stating the bride's taste and preferences and also helps avoid the embarrassment of two guests showing up with the same gift.

Wording and Style Depend on You — Some Examples:

Formal printed invitation:

Karen and Andrew Smith
invite you to attend a bridal shower
in honor of
Sue Miller and John Amaya
Saturday, June tenth at five o'clock
720 Maple Avenue
RSVP
(675) 568-3440
Kitchen and Bathroom Shower

Less formal bridal shower invitation:

You're invited to a couples bridal shower!
For: Andy Jacobs and Alice Martin
Date: Saturday, June 10th Time: 12:00 noon
Place: 720 El Medio Road
Newport Beach
Given by: Gail Robbins and Donna Cowen
RSVP (213) 494-7737 by May 25th
e-mail: doco@abc.com
It's a Handy Andy/Alice shower!
Flashlights with batteries and brooms are appropriate gifts!

The Creative Invitation

First impressions are important so choose your invitation carefully. It will set the mood for the theme and style of shower you have chosen. A unique and creative invitation is not only more fun to make but also more fun to receive. Use ribbons, stickers, rubber stamps, cords, and hand-made papers now readily available at your local craft and fine paper stores. Color themes make a dynamic impact. If the bride has a favorite color or is using a particular color in her future home, incorporate it into the shower invitation. It's great to capture the interest of your guests from the moment they read it!

Here are just a few ideas to spark your imagination:

Rain or Shine — Purchase either large fabric umbrellas or small paper ones (one for each guest invited) and a supply of fabric paints in complementary colors. Working with the umbrellas open, write the party details across a section of the material. When the paint is thoroughly dry, fold the umbrellas and slip them into cardboard tubes for mailing.

Postcards don't need envelopes and are less expensive to mail.

Sensational Tea — Cut out pictures of tea cups and tea pots, or purchase the readily-available stickers of tea cups and pots. Apply them to blank postcards or pieces of fine stationery folded in half to make a card. You can even pop in a foil-wrapped tea bag just to wet their appetite. Use a tea pot sticker to seal your envelope.

The Sweetheart Box — Each invitation will require a heart-shaped helium balloon (available at specialty and party stores), one yard of curling ribbon, and a white gift box slightly larger than the inflated balloon. Using colorful magic markers, write out the invitation on the balloon and tie a ribbon to it tightly. Tape the other end of the ribbon securely to the inside of the container. After your balloon "invitation" is nestled in the box, tape down the lid. These unique pop-up surprises should be hand-delivered to the doorstep of each guest.

Around-the-Clock Fun — In keeping with the theme of an Around-the-Clock shower (See Themes), cut individual alarm clocks out of colored fine art paper. You can use either a single sheet or a folded piece of paper, if you want the alarm clock to open. Write the shower details either on the back of each clock or inside, if you have chosen the folded style. Now you are ready to personalize the invitations. On each alarm clock, draw a face depicting a different time of day according to the time you've assigned each guest. These alarm clocks set the mood for the shower where each person brings a gift appropriate for the individually designated time of day.

Computers come with some great font styles. Use them to design your own shower invitation.

Kitchen Keepsake — For the kitchen shower, buy or make individual potholders or kitchen towels. Print out the shower information with fabric paint and you've just created a memorable addition to your friends' kitchens!

An Elegant Note — Select fine notecards and write out your invitation. If you or a friend know calligraphy, it can add to the overall elegance of your cards. Glue small satin bows in the top corners of the cards or punch two holes on the left hand side, thread a length of satin ribbon through each, and tie in a festive bow. Glitter or confetti scattered in the envelope will lend a festive air to your creation.

It's a Puzzle — Using your computer and scanner enlarge a picture of the happy couple to 5 x 7 inch or larger, and make enough copies to send one to each guest. Glue each picture onto a piece of foam core or thin white cardboard. When dry, write out the invitation on the back of each picture, then cut into irregular "puzzle" pieces. Each puzzle can be mailed in its own regular-size envelope.

A Night at the Movies — Headline your invitation with "When _____ Met _____. (Fill in the names of the bride and groom.) Embellish it with images of popcorn boxes, candy wrappers, videos, film titles, clapboards, and other movie-related items. Use words like "Starring," "Location," and "Call Time." Don't forget to check out the stickers at your favorite stationery or craft store. Let your imagination run wild.

Baker's Special — Bake oversized decorator cookies (See Personalized Initial Cookies) and write party details in frosting. This is a fun preview of a tea or dessert shower.

Sweet Temptation — As a prelude to a formal dessert party, buy quality chocolates specially packaged in tiny gold boxes. Make or order your invitations in black or white and gold to coordinate with the foil containers. Place each invitation on top of its own box and secure with a lacy gold ribbon.

The Delicate Touch — Buy individual fans to use as "cards" on which to write your summons to an Asian-themed shower.

Bon Voyage — A honeymoon shower needs a special invitation. Use fine art paper to fashion a travel ticket or select picture postcards to set the stage for your shower "adventure."

Linen Closet Cabaret — Use a linen or plain cloth napkin as a stunning background on which to paint the particulars of your linen or kitchen shower.

Creative Cut-Outs — Use beautiful hand printed or textured papers or scraps of eco fabrics to cut into shapes to suit your fancy. Hearts, bells, doves, flowers, stars, and initials of the bride and groom are just a few of the designs you can use to create a truly unique invitation that will complement your decorations.

Get a supply of already-stamped postcards from your post office to use as invitations of your own design.

Make a guest list and include name, address, telephone number(s), fax number and e-mail address.

2
PLANNING A BRIDAL SHOWER

ALL GOOD PARTIES involve work and the bridal shower is no exception! Planning a memorable party and having fun doing so should be your goal. Since a bridal shower takes the coordination of what may seem to be an endless number of small details, you need to start with a realistic assessment of your resources. Doing this before you begin makes the entire process easier and avoids unnecessary complications later on. First you need to decide what you can afford in terms of time and money. Then consider what other resources are available to you, including invaluables such as space, equipment, and talented or energetic friends! Knowing what you have to work with can help you begin to find the sort of celebration that is the perfect reflection of the guest of honor and your own personal style.

Setting the Date

Unless a surprise party is on the agenda, the hostess usually consults with the bride and perhaps the groom before finalizing the date. It's always preferable to have your guest of honor at the celebration! So, be sure to check before going ahead with a definite date.

Somewhere between four to six weeks prior to the wedding itself is a good time to hold a shower. This may vary according to individual schedules and the number of showers being held. In the case of several celebrations, be sure to double-check with the other hostesses or the bride herself to avoid planning your event for the same weekend as another party. Also, make sure that the time schedule you have set is realistic. Do you have enough time to prepare everything? Is there plenty of time to mail out the invitations with enough leeway for replies? Depending on the type of shower, you may need more time than you had originally planned on. Look at all the aspects, take possible scheduling conflicts into consideration, and then set a date that you can comfortably meet. Don't forget to think about the guests you will be inviting. If most of them work, a weekend luncheon might be easier to schedule than a party during the week. If most of the guests coming to an all-women shower are married, you might have a better turnout by selecting a weekday evening as opposed to a weekend evening when many couples have social obligations. That same weekend evening, however, is a great choice for a couples shower. It's a matter of knowing what type of shower you want and who you're inviting.

Choosing the Type of Shower and the Time of Day

Once you have set the date, you need to select an appropriate time of day. This is largely determined by the type of shower you will be giving, the guest list, and your budget.

First Things First:

- What's your estimated budget?
- How large do you want the party to be?
- Are you going to make it a couples shower?
- Look outside! How is the weather, warm or cold?
- Is it a surprise?

Working through the above should get you ready to sift through the various types of parties to find the one that best suits your style and circumstances.

Keep in mind both your expertise and your limitations. Plan a party that you can comfortably handle and will enjoy giving. If cooking is not your forté, it is wise not to commit yourself to a sitdown dinner for 40 unless you can afford to have it catered (you still get all the credit!). Once you've been realistic and carefully considered and established your limits, then you can get ready for the fun by letting your imagination and creativity safely run wild!

Types of Affairs and Their Appropriate Hours

A Breakfast Shower

Busy lives begin early, and a breakfast shower might be the perfect answer for either a weekday morning or a weekend rendezvous. During the week this type of shower can start as early as 7:30 AM. It can be held at your favorite breakfast spot or in the home. Generally speaking, a breakfast shower is a little less expensive.

A Brunch

Generally held on a weekend morning, a brunch is usually set for 10:00 or 11:00 AM and can be expected to last into the early afternoon. A good choice for both an all-female and a couples shower, a brunch can be either sit-down or buffet style. Often chosen because of its flexibility, this type of meal may take place indoors or out, being as formal or informal as you wish. Its versatility will accommodate even the most modest of budgets.

A Luncheon

Either a home or a restaurant is the appropriate setting for this type of event, which is usually slated to begin between noon and 1:00 PM. Whether offering table service or a buffet, which can be slightly cheaper, the cost is moderate to expensive.

An Afternoon Tea

Pressed for time? Whatever type of shower you choose to give, have the event fully or partially catered.

Usually set for between 2:00 and 5:00 PM, but commencing no later than 3:30 PM, this affair is best reserved for women friends. A tea is not only a delightful change of pace but also is relatively inexpensive.

A Cocktail Party

With its air of sophistication, the cocktail party is perfect for the couples celebration. It provides the ideal solution to space and budgetary limitations. You can do a lot with a little for this one!

Cocktails are served between 4:00 and 7:00 PM.

A Dinner Party

A dinner party can be quite versatile, everything from an all-ladies potluck buffet to an elegant sitdown dinner for couples. You can opt for either a weekday or weekend evening with a starting time anywhere from 5:00 to 7:00 PM. The cost will range from moderate to expensive.

A Dessert Party

Everyone loves sweets and there's no better place to indulge than at this tempting affair. A dessert party can be a mid-afternoon ladies gathering or a couples event starting after dinner, at 7:30 or 8:00 PM. It's fun, relatively inexpensive, and a sweet gesture for the couple-to-be!

Selecting a Location

In order to select a location that will enhance that special day, keep in mind the number of guests you want to invite, the type of party you want, the working budget, and the time of year. Also take into consideration any special locations you might have access to — country clubs, church halls, club meeting rooms, and local parks can all be kind to the limited budget.

Visit www.wedding location.com When you're looking for the perfect location for your shower, this is a great place to start.

Bridal showers hosted by co-workers and held in the office are increasingly popular. Many offices have kitchens in which to store and prepare foods, and a boardroom that can be decorated for the occasion.

Although most showers are given in the hostess's home, they may also be held in the home of the bride's mother or a relative, a restaurant or outdoor recreation area. Although a home tends to provide the coziest and most relaxed environment, a banquet room at a local hotel or club may be preferable for the larger shower. It's important to look objectively at the space you have in order to accurately estimate how many people you can comfortably entertain. If your guests primarily will be standing, as in the case of a cocktail party, the average room can generally accommodate 20 guests. A three-room area consisting of living, dining and family rooms can hold about forty. Plan on rearranging furniture and removing bulky items temporarily to allow for a smooth flow of guests from one room to the next. This assures that the guests can mingle freely without traffic jams and tight corners. If you're planning on a buffet brunch, don't forget to consider available seating.

Be creative and flexible when it comes to looking at your options. Try to find a location that enhances the theme of your shower, rather than remaining a neutral backdrop. On the other hand, be willing to adjust your theme to fit a great location. If you're holding a summer shower and your choice of locations has been narrowed down to the beach or local park, why not enhance the setting by opting for a Hawaiian luau or Western barbecue? Try to utilize the community you live in by checking with your local Parks and Recreation Authority for available sites. Before settling on one, however, make sure that you are up-to-date on whether a permit is required, if fires and alcoholic beverages are allowed, and how parking and traffic are managed. Another great resource is your local historical society. Just imagine staging an Elegant Afternoon Tea in the quaint garden of a Victorian

If you're giving the bride-to-be a shower at the office, ask a co-worker to help with coordinating the affair.

mansion or an English cottage. The possibilities are endless; it just takes a little legwork to locate your options.

In making a final decision on location, keep the overall budget in mind. A home shower, whether indoors or out in the garden, will be less costly than one held at a club or restaurant.

Determining Your Budget

A good place to start, if you're hosting the shower yourself, is by taking a careful look at your own finances. What can you comfortably afford to spend? With the knowledge of your location and the length of your guest list, begin by writing down everything you think you will need to carry off the event you're planning. Use the shower checklist provided on page 31 to make sure you haven't overlooked a small but costly detail. If you see that you are beginning to leave your original budget far behind, stop and regroup! Budgets can be saved! You can cut down on the number of guests or modify the style of the shower. For example, if you had *If your budget allows, hire an event-planner to fulfill your fantasy of a perfect bridal shower. (No one ever said that "time-savers" were "money-savers!")* planned on hosting a sitdown luncheon calling for the rental of tables, linens, and chairs, consider changing to an afternoon tea serving dainty finger sandwiches and desserts, where only napkins or small paper plates are necessary.

The best way to work on a limited budget is to have a co-hostess (even better, if it is the entire bridal party!). Have a general meeting to determine the budget and divide the responsibilities. The money can be pooled with one or two people acting as the shoppers for items the group has already agreed upon, or each person can be assigned things to purchase. Either way, be sure to write down who's responsible for what to avoid confusion as you get closer to the date.

Try to keep costs to a minimum by borrowing things you don't have from a friend. Rather than renting china, feel free to use the beautiful paper or plastic plates available at your local party goods store.

Budget Tips
- Hold the party at your home or in a friend's patio or garden.
- Decide on a breakfast shower, brunch, afternoon tea, or dessert party.
- Buy food and/or liquor from a wholesale outlet.
- Eliminate alcohol in favor of exotic fruit punch.
- Hire students, 21 years or older, of course, to help set up, serve, and tend bar.
- When going formal, check with your local hotel and restaurant management school for competent but less expensive waiters, bartenders, and catering help.
- Create your own floral arrangement or centerpieces, concentrating on the flowers currently in season. In winter, choose dried flowers for centerpieces.
- Balloons can be the budget decorator's best friend — colorful and versatile, they won't deplete your finances!

3
Secrets
for a Successful
Bridal Shower

*T*HE SECRET to a successful party is all in the organization. Let a few tips be your guide to making your shower the best and most enjoyable it can possibly be! And remember, by doing things in time, you will be the best kind of hostess there is — a relaxed one!

Shower Tips

General Tips to Get You Going

- ~ Go with the kind of party you do best. As simple as this seems, many hostesses get carried away and end up over their heads with a party that just isn't feasible. Accept your limitations and respect your budget, the size of your locale, and the availability of equipment and help.

~ Don't just admire the checklist and worksheets provided, use them! Rely on your pencil and not on your memory—write it down!!

~ Follow the shower checklist furnished on page 31 as your master plan to avoid leaving things to the very last minute.

~ Check silver, linens, and any necessary supplies well ahead of time.

~ Go over the seating possibilities, and make sure that you have enough chairs and space for the number of guests.

~ Consider choosing a party theme. Theme celebrations are usually fun and definitely more memorable. (See Chapter on Themes.)

 If you employ a housekeeper, hire her (or him) to help with the clean-up after your party is over.

Now-that-you're-on-your-way

~ If you have chosen a theme, coordinate the invitations, food, decorations, and party favors. You want your theme to be a focal point, not merely an afterthought.

~ Try to invite guests who know each other or at least one other person. Otherwise there will be too much pressure on you (and the guest of honor) during the party.

~ Plan games and activities that will appeal to your guests. Games can turn an ordinary party into a special event.

~ Select party favors that are different. Unusual and hand-made items are more fun for your guests.

~ If you think you will need help to carry off the party with style, by all means, get it! Ask a friend or turn to one of the many professional agencies for special help. Students can also be your saving grace when it comes to food preparation, serving, and cleanup.

~ Plan on keeping the menu manageable so that you will be free to enjoy yourself along with your guests! Stay away from time-consuming dishes and remember, this is NOT the time to experiment, no matter what your Aunt Tilly says!

~ In calculating the amount of food you will need, overestimate cheerfully. It's always better to have leftovers than to run short. To prevent food from getting cold, plan on borrowing or renting chafing dishes and hot plates.

Basics Not To Forget

~ If you can afford it, single-use 35mm cameras with flash are a must, as is the camcorder or digital video camera.

~ Buy film for your camera and camcorder ahead of time.

~ Assign the role of photographer to someone who knows which end of the camera should be facing forward. Chances are you yourself will get sidetracked. Terrific shots can later be made into a special momento for the bride.

~ Have your guest bathroom well-stocked with the niceties party-goers appreciate — guest soaps, hand towels, lotion, and an extra roll of toilet tissue.

~ Make your powder room special by adding fresh flowers, scented potpourri, and, for evening, a lit candle, to make your guests feel pampered.

~ Get all of the cleaning and most of the cooking out of the way ahead of time, and try not to leave anything until the last minute.

Choose ready-made or frozen food items from your local supermarket to serve to the guests. There are many specialty foods now available to impress the most discerning connoisseur.

More Basics Closer to the Date

- If you are having a large gathering, hire a valet parking service to park the cars of your guests.

- Decide now if you want to give the bride a corsage since it must be ordered in advance.

- Select a "gift corner" where the bride will be able to sit comfortably in full view of all her friends as she opens her gifts.

- Plan seating so that it will help, not hinder, conversation.

- If you are serving buffet-style, be sure to scatter tray tables around the room or give each guest a lap tray for her food.

- Inexpensive but charming wicker lap trays can be purchased for each guest and then given as a favor to take home.

- Be a little daring in your seating arrangement for a sit-down dinner. Separate spouses, placing each one next to someone new.

- Choose creative ways to serve your food to add a festive note to your table (See Table Settings.)

- Create the atmosphere you want through the skillful use of lighting, music, and decorations. Whether lively, elegant, or cozy, there's a mood to fit your party — experiment with the options in advance until you hit on the right combination.

- Smoothly-run parties have definite stages that can be planned in advance. Be aware of the time and how your guests are feeling as indications that they may be ready for the next stage.

- The beginning of a party can be awkward. Ask a few close friends to arrive early so that the first guest steps into a lively atmosphere.

- Above all, be prepared, so that when the guests arrive, you at least look relaxed.

Depending on the size of your gathering and where it will be held, you may want to employ servers, bartenders, even an entertainer.

SHOWER CHECKLIST

Six to Eight Weeks Before

- ☐ Discuss your plans for hosting a shower with the bride. Go over the guest list, date and theme.
- ☐ If it's a surprise shower, contact the bride's mother and fiancé to let them know your plans and to obtain the wedding guest list.
- ☐ Once the date is set, be sure that the bride's mother, the groom, and anyone else involved in planning the shower knows the chosen date and time.
- ☐ If there is more than one hostess, hold a meeting to discuss theme, location, and budget, and to divide the duties.
- ☐ Draw up the guest list.
- ☐ If it is not an at-home affair, look for a banquet room at a hotel, restaurant, or club and reserve it immediately (this may require a deposit).
- ☐ Set a preliminary budget so that you have something to work with.
- ☐ Decide on a theme and the type and style of the shower you want to host.
- ☐ Make or buy appropriate invitations.
- ☑ Fill out the invitations and address the envelopes. Include an RSVP date, which should be one to two weeks prior to the event. Be sure you have given a telephone number.
- ☐ Think about decorating ideas and start browsing to see what's available. Good party supply and art stores are filled with great party items. Check rental companies, the yellow pages, and use your imagination for further ideas.
- ☐ If this is a joint shower, divide the decorating tasks and expenses. Deciding who will be responsible for doing what is almost as crucial as actually doing it!
- ☐ If you're using party help, reserve early — caterers, servers, and clean-up help can get booked up far in advance, especially during holiday seasons.

☐ Think about having entertainment. If you want to hire musicians, palm readers, magicians, or other entertainers, it is wise to find and book them immediately.

☐ If games are on the agenda, decide on which ones and start collecting everything you need.

Four to Six Weeks Before

☐ Determine the number and type of game prizes needed and start shopping for them.

☐ Purchase or make your party favors.

☐ Set your menu and gather the recipes needed.

☐ Begin your checklist of necessary equipment, food, and liquor.

☐ Reserve rental items.

☐ Purchase or make place cards. As soon as guests begin to confirm, fill in their names on the cards.

☐ Mail out the invitations (four weeks before).

Three Weeks Before

☐ If there are other hostesses involved, call another meeting to check on everyone's progress and to assign food and beverage preparation chores.

☐ Make a detailed marketing list for food.

☐ Finish shopping for game equipment and prizes.

☐ Put the finishing touches on party favors, if necessary.

Two Weeks Before

☐ Assign a shower secretary to be in charge of recording who brought which gift. The same person can also make a ribbon "bridal bouquet" for the bride.

☐ Do all major cleaning, such as emptying coat closets.

☐ If the event is being held in a hotel or club, confirm your reservation. Also, finalize the menu with the staff coordinator.

☐ Order floral centerpieces.

☐ Touch base with the entertainers and caterers — or friends who have promised to bring food.

☐ Wrap game prizes.

One Week Before

☐ Tally up the number of guests and call those who have not yet responded to see if they are planning to attend. This is especially critical for a sitdown meal.

☐ Arrange for valet parking.

☐ Prepare food that can be frozen ahead of time.

☐ Start decorating.

☐ Decide what you will wear and make sure that it is cleaned and pressed.

☐ Clean and polish the silver.

☐ Arrange for space in a neighbor's refrigerator, if needed.

☐ Clean the house.

Two Days Before

☐ Review the checklist to make sure that nothing has been overlooked.

☐ Check with the other hostesses to make sure that things have gone smoothly for them.

☐ Confirm delivery or pickup time with your florist. Delivery should be set for early in the morning of your event.

☐ Collect everything you need to borrow — chairs, tables, and serving pieces.

☐ Make sure that all linens are ironed.

☐ Wash china and crystal.

The Day Before

- [ ] Make any food that can be safely stored overnight. Some foods, such as pasta salads, are actually better when made the day before.
- [ ] Clean the fruit and vegetables and get them ready for slicing.
- [ ] Recheck the delivery time of rental items.
- [ ] Set up chairs, tables with linens, and get out serving utensils and napkins.
- [ ] Finish last-minute decorating and straightening up around the house.
- [ ] Make sure you have enough ice.
- [ ] Pick up flowers late in the day unless they are scheduled to be delivered the next morning.
- [ ] Set up an area to display the shower gifts.
- [ ] Last but not least — take a hot bath, relax, and get a good night's sleep!

The Day of the Shower

- [ ] Have another hostess or friend come early to help with last-minute details.
- [ ] Finish preparing the food.
- [ ] Make punches, juices, etc.
- [ ] Place food on serving dishes and garnish.
- [ ] Get dressed.
- [ ] If serving snack or finger foods like nuts, chips and dip, or cheese and crackers, set them out just before your guests are scheduled to arrive.

The Party Itself

- [ ] Greet your guests with a smile, an offer of a drink, and introduce them to at least one other person.
- [ ] If this is a surprise shower, have the bride arrive a half hour after all the other guests. Appoint someone as lookout and get ready to shout "surprise! "

☐ When the bride makes her entrance, greet her with a corsage, lei, or other special favor you have planned for her.

☐ Proceed according to the timetable you have already planned.

☐ Remember to be aware of the time and the mood of the guests in deciding when to move onto the next activity. Do not rush your guests but don't leave them waiting and wondering what's next, either.

☐ Help the bride put her presents in her car.

☐ When the shower is being held at a restaurant, hotel, or club, plan on arriving in plenty of time to make any final arrangements. Count on doing last minute decorating, setting out place cards, arranging party favors, and being finished in enough time to greet the first guest with a smile!

Shower Timetable

It's important to keep your party flowing so that it doesn't begin to drag. A slow pace can become boring, making the guests begin to get restless. Think of your party in three stages, allowing approximately 30 minutes to one hour for each. The exact length will depend on your guests.

First Stage

As guests arrive, introduce them to one another and serve drinks. You may want to have a few hors d'oeuvres, nuts or candies, but keep the snacks light so as not to spoil the meal! Although this is the time to socialize, while waiting for everyone to arrive, you may want to start a quick game. Some games will be better suited than others but all will help break the ice and get people interacting.

Second Stage

This is when the food is served. If it is a complete meal, it is up to you whether you want to serve dessert immediately following or wait until after the gifts have been opened.

Third Stage

Now is the time for any games you might have planned. Activities can be a lot of fun and can make a good party great! In case there are too many guests and you feel that opening the presents will take a long time, you may want to skip having games or select ones to be played only in the first stage of the party. If you have not yet served coffee and cake, either have guests enjoy it while the presents are being opened or wait until the guest of honor has opened all her gifts.

Enlist the help of friends or hire the staff you need for a successful bridal shower. They can even help polish the silver.

Party favors that are not part of the place setting are given to the guests as they are preparing to leave. You can have them ready on a small table in the entrance hall.

4
DECORATIONS AND TABLE SETTINGS

ECORATIONS AND TABLE SETTINGS are vital to the mood and character of any festivity, so both should be carefully planned to complement the theme and style of your party. Decorations can run the gamut from very simple to extremely elaborate. What is important is the continuity of style.

Parties are really theatrical productions and you are the director. Decide how you want the stage to look and choose an appropriate setting, a delicious menu, interesting accessories and entertainment, add the spice of fun loving guests, and you are guaranteed to have a smash success on your hands!

Decorating with Imagination

Indulge your imagination to create just the right atmosphere. If you prefer a formal, elegant style of shower without a particular theme, then beautiful flowers, candles, linens, and food arrangements can tastefully convey an atmosphere of sophisticated refinement. If, on the other hand, you're in search of an informal, comfortable setting for a "Sushi Party" you may want to create an Asian theme. Use bamboo or silk fan-like placemats, provide each guest with a pair of chopsticks monogrammed with the couples names, get ginger-scented candles embellished with calligraphy to use as centerpieces, put up travel posters of Japan, and decorate the room with red and black lacquer containers filled with floating candles, flowers, and fruit. Cover large serving trays with a mouthwatering array of sushi and sashimi decorated with tiny umbrellas. Add the crowning touch by playing Japanese music in the background or having a live cellist perform the silken-tone of her instrument for guests. And don't forget the fortune cookies.

If you're holding the wedding shower at a restaurant, ask the owner or events coordinator what they have in the way of centerpieces and decorations so you can work around their items. This will save a lot of time and effort on your part.

Get into the real spirit and dress the part! You and/or your help can dress appropriately for the theme you've chosen. For a sushi party, clothe yourself and your help in kimonos to become part of the decorating atmosphere. Other themes might require Victorian, Italian, Mexican or Hawaiian attire. Use things that you have around the house, or pick up inexpensive items at local thrift stores. For an elegant cocktail or dinner party, ask the help to dress in black skirts or pants with crisp white shirts.

Keep in mind that decorating is not just balloons and banners, it encompasses everything found at the party. The centerpiece, linens, and dishes you choose are enhanced by the way you fold the napkins and display the food on the buffet table. Whether you place them at each place setting or reserve them for later, your party favors are a not-to-be-forgotten decorating must. The following information is designed to give you ideas so that you can find just the right combination to create that special shower. Feel free to mix and match ideas to get the final look you're after.

Decorating Delights

Balloons — Always fun and festive, these light-hearted charmers can be relied on to create a colorful entrance. You can also attach streamers and let them dangle as the balloons float up to the ceiling. Or use the colorful ties to secure them to the back of each chair, a wine glass or napkin ring.

Banners and Streamers — Printed with congratulations or the couples names, these make a dramatic statement stretched across an entry way or crisscrossing a room.

Flowers and Plants — Greenery can be just the right touch in creating a simple but striking centerpiece or transforming a room into a lush tropical paradise. Be creative with vases of flowers — put lemons or oranges in bowls and vases to hold the flowers in place. Scrunched up cellophane creates the look of ice.

Flower Pots — Use the contemporary lightweight flower pots that come with great designs, or consider sponging plain pots and filling them with flowering plants. Let guests take them home as favors.

Candles — For evening showers, candles offer many ways to create decorations. Try wrapping a grapevine leaf around short candles and tying them with raffia. Slender candles can be anchored in small dishes with marbles or pebbles. "Luminaries"— candles set in sand in brown paper lunch bags — are especially captivating and you can add to their effect by punching holes along the top edges of the paper bags. These are excellent for showers held outdoors.

Designer Shopping Bags — These come in fabulous colors and designs, with or without handles. Fill them with colored tissue paper, iridescent cellophane, or shredded paper filling. Stuff individual bags with favors for the guests and place at each table setting.

Travel Posters — Place travel posters around the room to make your guests feel as if they've arrived at your theme location or the couples honeymoon destination.

Hats — Mexican sombreros, chefs' hats, cowboy hats, embroidered caps or vintage Victorian bonnets can easily be incorporated into distinctive table displays. If the wedding shower has no particular theme, invite your guests to wear a favorite hat. Many individuals have hats but not too many opportunities to wear them. Brunch, lunch, tea, and cocktail showers lend themselves to dressing up!

Piñatas — Mexican streamers and pinatas make wonderful decorations. They come in many different shapes and colors and are easy to find.

English-Style Crackers — A decoration that "snaps" when two people pull to open. Crackers are now available in many stores and provide a fun way to share a joke or saying.

Napkins and Napkin Holders — Rolled or fanned napkins look fabulous tied with a colorful wide or narrow ribbon. For added flair, tie with a piece of ivy and tuck in a rose or other seasonal bloom.

If your shower falls near a holiday, you may want to decorate around that holiday theme. Valentine's Day calls for red hearts, white doilies, heart-shaped candle holders and napkins secured with heart-shaped cookies cutters that can also serve as favors. Easter needs rabbits and chocolate or marshmallow eggs, while Halloween begs for a pumpkin centerpiece. Halloween is also the perfect holiday for caramel and chocolate covered apples wrapped in cellophane and tied with orange and black curling ribbon. Thanksgiving and Christmas both deserve holiday decorations with chocolate turkeys or glittery Christmas ornaments for party favors.

Go to your favorite supermarket for a one-stop shopping spree. You'll most likely find everything from food and beverages to balloons to paper goods to flowers and candles. You might even find a centerpiece item on sale or something for favors. What could be easier, just add them to the cart!

As you consider special holidays, remember the celebrations and/or restrictions that might affect your shower date — for example, Kwanza, Cinco de Mayo, Tet, Ramadan, Passover, Yom Kippur, Hannukah, Mardi Gras and so on.

The Perfect Centerpiece

The centerpiece is deservedly the focal point of the table, and, as such, should coordinate with and complement the rest of the setting. Flowers are by far the most popular choice of centerpieces. Coming in a wide variety of shapes and sizes, floral arrangements are prized for their ability to add the freshness of color to any table setting. Arrange the blossoms you choose loosely in a favorite vase or secure with marbles or rocks. Take care that your arrangement is not distracting to those who will be seated directly in front of it. Flowers should be positioned so that they are either above or below eye level so as not to obstruct someone's view. As you are adjusting the centerpiece, take the time to step back from the table and look at the bouquet in terms of the overall effect. How high is the ceiling? When it's high, you should opt for a more grandiose spray that can hold its own and not get lost in the room. How wide is the table? You don't want to create an overpowering arrangement.

Small flowers can be artfully grouped in separate glass bowls which, when pushed together, give the illusion of one sweeping arrangement. At the end of the shower, give each guest her own bowl of blossoms to take home.

It is easier and more economical to select flowers that are in season. Exotic flowers can be beautiful and expensive so be sure you know the cost before settling on your final arrangement. Keep your color scheme in mind while making your selection, and don't be afraid to add a little "spice" to your decorating scheme.

Bouquets can be ordered directly from the florist or you can create them yourself, depending on your budget, time, and talent. When opting to make your own arrangements, be creative in your choice of containers. Your fragrant centerpiece can become delightfully different by being arranged in crystal vases, decorative boxes, ceramic pots, or woven baskets. It's helpful to use a piece of "green oasis" in the bottom of the container so that the flowers have water while being held securely where you place them.

A more casual look for a barbecue with a gardening theme can be achieved by arranging live potted flowers as a centerpiece. You can either paint the pots or cover them in a pretty fabric tied with a bow. Give the pots to the bride at the end of the shower or plant them in your garden as a lovely reminder of a very special day.

An evening affair can be enhanced by a centerpiece which incorporates votive candles. A mirror can be used as a reflective base on which to set your flowers surrounded by flickering candles. A beautiful alternative is to place slender tapers on either side of the floral display.

When it comes to choosing a centerpiece, don't think just in terms of floral arrangements. There is virtually no limit to the variety of interesting and striking items that can be used to grace the center of your party table.

Just for Variety Centerpieces

Beach Bucket — Fill to overflowing with tropical flowers to add fragrance to your Hawaiian luau or beach party.

Umbrellas — Intertwine pink and white ribbons around the handles of miniature umbrellas to hold fresh flowers in place.

Candles — Floating candles are very elegant. They come in an array of colors and can be floated in clear glass bowls for a stunning effect.

Balloons — Attach a helium balloon bouquet to a basket filled with flowers, candy or stuffed animals. Balloons now come in many sizes and shapes — just check out the local gift and grocery stores for ideas.

Food — Delight all the senses with an edible centerpiece. A luscious dessert surrounded by colorful blossoms, oversized strawberries piled haphazardly on a silver tray, or a tempting array of fresh fruit carefully arranged in a basket all make a feast for the eyes, as well as the palate.

Chocolate Swans — Let large chocolate swans grace your table.

Their hollowed-out backs can be filled with truffles or chocolate-dipped strawberries.

Chocolate Roses — Give into a fabulous spray of chocolate roses, either solo or interspersed with fresh flowers. Present each guest with this long-stemmed delicacy when the celebration is over.

These are just a few ideas that I hope will encourage you to use your imagination when creating your own wonderful centerpiece or adding that very special touch to a scrumptious buffet table. There's very little effort involved and it's well worth the time spent on your own flights of fancy to come up with the touch that is unmistakably "you."

A Beautiful Buffet Table

You may have items around your house that you can use as decoration. Perhaps you can find a set of miniature twinkle lights to create a sparkling romantic wonderland for the couples shower.

A buffet table can be a visual treat when the food is well-displayed and tastefully arranged in appropriate serving dishes that are imaginatively garnished. Where the food is placed can either add to or detract from the desired effect. Enhance the theme you've chosen through your selection of linens and serving pieces. If the table is crowded you may have to forego other decorations or reduce the size of your centerpiece.

Since most of the lavish effect of a buffet comes from the food, find creative ways of laying out the feast. Also be sure that you have planned for a sufficient number of serving pieces in the size and type you'll need.

Serving Pieces with Savvy

- Crystal bowls or plates for a formal affair.
- Silver trays and platters add a ceremonial air.
- Baskets lined with real or designer paper napkins add color and style for holding muffins and breads.
- Decorative boxes and tins give a unique flair.
- Hollowed-out watermelons, pineapples, and papayas are perfect for displaying fruit salads.
- Champagne or parfait glasses are great for serving desserts.
- Festive fiesta-ware for a backyard barbeque.
- Hollowed-out cabbages or artichokes for dips.
- Chafing dishes to keep food piping hot at a buffet-style shower.
- Stainless steel and modern brightly colored plastic bowls and tableware for a high-tech shower.
- Fondue pots for serving hot meatballs, or chocolate for dipping fruits.

From Plain to Gorgeous — Making Food a Feast for the Eyes

After you have gathered all the basics (serving pieces, trays, etc.), it's time to concentrate on the little touches that will give your buffet table pizzazz. The way you present the food is of utmost importance. Doilies, lettuce or kale leaves can be used to line dishes and platters. Sprigs of parsley or mint are meant for those small corners that need a special touch. Lemons, limes, and oranges thinly sliced are perfect for trimming a tray. Also, reach for grapes and strawberries, as well as fresh flowers to complete your platters.

Make your food presentation as eye-appealing as possible. Look at the texture and color of the food, as well as how it goes with the other dishes being served. The way you cut or don't cut the food can also add interest and appeal. Vary the size, and when looking for a dramatic look, use whole pieces — giant strawberries dipped in chocolate are stunning as a dessert. Huge mushrooms stuffed with a tasty filling can be placed side-by-side with whole baby carrots on a tray.

Pay careful attention to the way you arrange the food. Cheese, for example, should be displayed on a cheese board or lovely platter. Place a large uncut portion of the cheese in the back or center and surround with small slices. Use a hollowed-out cabbage or artichoke as a colorful container for dip. Set it in the center of a large tray with cut vegetables encircling it. Arrange food, like stuffed snow peas, cookies, or slices of nut bread by overlapping individual pieces in concentric rings.

Table Settings with Style

An empty table comes to life as it is filled with the items you enjoy. Pay close attention to even the smallest detail when creating your table, carefully selecting the right type of table covering, plates, glasses, utensils, and napkins in order to attain the mood you want. Keep in mind that your table should be harmonious. Choose tablecloths that coordinate with your dishes and the style of the party. Achieve a new look by layering different fabrics in either coordinating or contrasting color combinations. Placemats may be the right choice for the casual table. For an elegant shower, use napkins to create a distinctive place setting. Fold into a fan shape and tuck into a goblet, or simply tie each with

Doilies are a quick and easy way to add style to your surroundings. Use them under plates and vases, or use them to wrap up dainty flowers to put at each place setting. Doilies are especially apropos for An Elegant Afternoon Tea.

an elegant bow. For a slightly less formal look, a large napkin can be tied into a loose knot or dressed up with a napkin ring and placed directly on each plate.

More Ideas for Stylish Settings

Buffet without Table Seating

- ~ Charming tray tables should be strategically placed throughout the room to give guests a place to set their drinks.
- ~ Purchase individual bamboo lap trays for everyone. They can be decorated and given as party favors or saved for future occasions.
- ~ China, paper, or plastic plates are all appropriate for this type of shower. Plates should be stacked at the beginning of the buffet line.
- ~ When deciding on paper or plastic plates, choose sturdy ones among the widely available designer styles.
- ~ With china, always use stainless or sterling flatware. If you are using paper plates, good plastic utensils or your stainless is fine.
- ~ Napkins and flatware should be placed together, either next to the plates or at the end of the buffet. There are a number of ways to arrange the silverware. Choose to line it up neatly or roll each set in a napkin, tie with a bow, and place in a beautiful basket or silverware caddy. You can also use a large napkin to tie around each set of utensils, which is then stacked on the table or in a basket.
- ~ Wine, champagne or punch should already be poured and waiting in glasses at the end of the buffet line. If space is at a premium, move the beverages to another area.
- ~ Party favors should be distributed as your guests are leaving.

Buffet with Table Seating

- ~ Count, count, and recount! Make sure that you have an adequate number of tables and chairs, which can be either rented or borrowed.

- ~ Select a colorful tablecloth, whether linen or paper. Linens in a number of lovely shades can be obtained from party rental stores.

- ~ Linen napkins to match or coordinate with the tablecloth are a must for the elegant buffet. For a less formal look, there is a wide selection of paper tablecloths with matching napkins to choose from at your local party supply store. Browse with your budget and style in mind!

- ~ This type of buffet allows the utensils to be positioned next to the plates, at the end of the buffet or in a regular place setting at each table. No matter which you choose, always place the napkin with the silverware.

- ~ Fold each napkin in half and place to the left of each plate with the utensils on top, or add the magic of folding it in a special way. What you do with the napkin and where you place it can add life to your table.

- ~ For the casual luncheon with a kitchen theme, turn to scarfs, bandannas, or kitchen towels for napkins and placemats. These eyecatchers can then be taken home by your guests.

- ~ Open seating for this type of party is the easiest, but you may want to add a more personal note by using place cards. Choose a style that you feel drawn to and reflects the theme of your party.

- ~ An element of surprise adds sparkle so treat your guests to a special party favor at each place setting. Many party favors can double as place cards. (See Party Favors.)

- ~ If you are setting the individual tables, set out the wine and water goblets as well. Water glasses should be filled before the guests are seated. An open bottle of wine may be placed at each table for the guests to serve themselves.

A Sit-down Meal

~ In calculating the seating, don't forget to count yourself and the guest of honor! It's always wise to have a few additional chairs in the event of an additional, last-minute guest.

~ Linen tablecloths and napkins should definitely be part of your table on this formal occasion. Although white is always appropriate, you may opt for colored linens to complement your china and decor. Consider layering your linens to add color and variety.

~ For this gathering, it's time to bring out your best china, crystal, and silver. If you don't own an elegant service, don't worry, just turn to your local rental company (this may mean Mom). If you're going to be borrowing the china from several loving relatives, either alternate the different patterns at each place setting or set different tables with their own complete pattern.

~ Creating napkins of distinction will turn the ordinary table into a spectacular one. Whether adhering to the simplicity of an elegantly-folded napkin by itself or choosing the adornment of a beautiful rose, you should choose a napkin that makes a statement. Surprise your guests by using a party favor to embellish each napkin. Your innovative creations can then be placed to the left of the cutlery or on top of the plates.

~ Have your table completely set before the first celebrant arrives. Water glasses are filled just before the guests are seated. Leave guests to serve their own wine from an elegant decanter placed on the table or have a waiter circulate with the wine after all are seated.

Napkin Folding With Flair

Napkin Roll

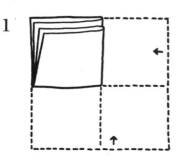 

1. With right side down, fold into quarters.

2. Place utensils on napkin.

3. Roll napkin around utensils, secure with a ribbon.

The Tulip

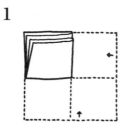 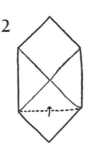  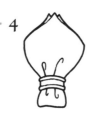

1. With right side down, fold into quarters.

2. Fold left and right corners into center.

3. Fold bottom corner up to center.

4. Turn over with point up, slip on napkin ring.

Fan Fold in Goblet

   1. Fold napkin in half.

   2. Pleat in one-inch accordion pleats from one end to the other.

   3. Place one end into a goblet and allow the other to open.

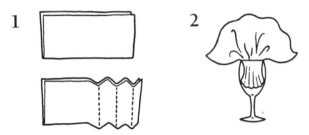

Folded Napkin

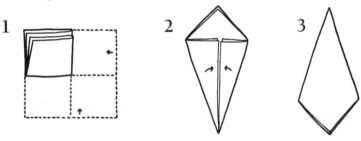

   1. With right side down, fold into quarters.

   2. Fold left and right corners into center.

   3. Turn the napkin over and lay it flat with top pointing up or down.

Fan Fold with Ribbon

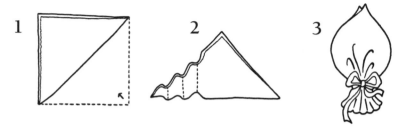

1. Fold napkin in half, diagonally.
2. Pleat in one-inch accordion pleats from one end to the other.
3. Secure with a ribbon a couple of inches up from bottom edge.
4. Lay flat, allowing top to open.

Rolled Napkin

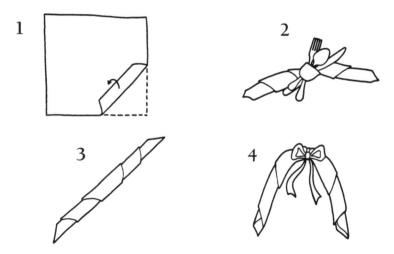

1. Lay napkin out right side down.
2. Roll diagonally from bottom right to upper left.
3. Tie napkin in a knot around utensils, or tie a ribbon around the center of napkin; lay flat in crescent shape.

5
A Festive Brunch

VARIETY is the spice of life and there's no better place to demonstrate this than at an informal brunch. Start your lazy Saturday or Sunday off the right way by beginning your shower at 10:30 or 11:00 AM. Let your guests slowly wake up to a tempting array of tantalizing dishes that can be prepared easily and inexpensively in advance. The number of entrees you decide on is up to you — browse through the following menues for ideas.

Quiches and Belgian Waffles

Menu

Fresh Fruit Salad   *Broccoli and Tomato Quiche*
Belgian Waffle and Sausage
Assorted Muffins and Coffee Cake
Mimosas   *White Wine*
Specialty Coffee and Teas

Fresh Fruit Salad

Create a stunning centerpiece by choosing to serve this refreshing treat in a hollowed-out watermelon or create individual fruit cups by filling empty orange or cantaloupe halves. Prepare the salad by slicing, cubing, and scooping out small balls of any combination of the following:

cantaloupe or honeydew melon

oranges

tangerines

bananas

apples

pineapple

strawberries

grapes

Note: Be sure to dip apples and bananas in lemon juice to prevent them from darkening. To keep these two fruits from becoming mushy, add them to the salad just before serving.

Broccoli and Tomato Quiche

1	*9" pastry shell, partially baked*
5	*eggs*
1½	*cups grated cheese, sharp Cheddar, Monterey Jack or a combination of the two*
¾	*pint plain yogurt*
1	*small head broccoli, broken into florets*
1	*large tomato, diced*
4	*green onions, diced*

¼   *teaspoon salt*

⅛   *teaspoon pepper*

In a large bowl, beat eggs and yogurt together. Mix in salt and pepper and set aside. Sprinkle half of the grated cheese over the bottom of the pastry shell. Arrange the broccoli over the cheese, distributing evenly. Spread the green onions and diced tomatoes over the broccoli, cover with the remaining cheese. Pour the egg and yogurt mixture over all. Bake at 375° for 40–45 minutes or until the center is solid.

Serves 8

Belgian Waffles

4   *eggs, separated*

2   *tablespoons granulated sugar*

½   *teaspoon salt*

1   *cup milk*

½   *teaspoon vanilla*

4   *tablespoons butter or margarine, melted and cooled*

1   *cup all-purpose flour*
      melted butter or margarine
      powdered sugar
      sweetened whipped cream
      strawberries, whole or sliced

In a medium bowl, beat egg whites just until stiff, set aside. In a large bowl, combine egg yolks, sugar, and salt, and beat until thick. Blend in milk, vanilla, and 4 tablespoons butter. While continuing to beat, add flour and blend well. Gently fold in egg whites.

Preheat Belgian waffle iron according to manufacturer's directions and brush with butter if required. Pour recommended amount of batter onto waffle iron, spreading evenly to cover grids. Bake according to printed instructions. To serve, let waffle cool slightly and dust with powdered sugar before topping with whipped cream and strawberries. Serve with cooked sausage links or bacon on the side. For a more health-conscious approach, check your supermarket for the savory non-pork sausages and turkey bacon now widely available.

To keep the buffet line moving, borrow an additional iron from a friend and have a helper start making waffles before the guests sit down.

Makes 5 waffles

Muffins and Coffee Cake

Let the tantalizing aroma of freshly baked goods complement your brunch. Present these delicious crowd pleasers on a tray or piled in a basket. Purchased croissants or bagels should come from a bakery specializing in these delicacies to insure their freshness.

Apple Muffins

1	*egg, beaten*
1	*cup milk*
4	*tablespoons vegetable oil*
2	*cups sifted flour*
4	*teaspoons baking powder*
½	*teaspoon salt*
2	*tablespoons sugar*
1	*cup sweetened applesauce*

Combine egg with milk and vegetable oil. Sift flour together with baking powder, salt, and sugar. Stir lightly into milk and egg mixture, mixing only until flour is dampened. Using a greased muffin tin, drop just enough batter into each cup to cover the bottom. Spread a rounded teaspoon of applesauce over batter and fill sections three fourths full with remaining batter. Bake at 375° for approximately 25 minutes or until toothpick inserted comes out dry.

Makes 12 small or 6 large muffins

Blueberry Crumb Muffins

¼   *cup shortening*
¼   *cup sugar*
1   *egg, well beaten*
1   *cup sifted flour*
3   *teaspoons baking powder*
½   *teaspoon salt*
1   *cup fine dry bread crumbs*
1   *cup milk*
1   *cup fresh blueberries (substitute frozen if needed)*

Cream the shortening and sugar together until light. Stir in the well-beaten egg. Sift together flour, baking powder, and salt, and add bread crumbs. Combine crumbs with the creamed mixture by thirds, alternating with milk. Lightly stir in the blueberries being careful not to crush them. Ladle into well-greased muffin pans, filling them about two-thirds full. Bake at 375° for 25 minutes, testing with a toothpick to check if baked.

Makes 12 medium-sized muffins

Pecan Sour Cream Coffee Cake

½	cup butter or margarine
1	cup granulated sugar
3	eggs
2	cups sifted flour
1	teaspoon baking powder
1	teaspoon baking soda
¼	teaspoon salt
1	cup sour cream
½	cup raisins

Pecan Topping:

¾	cup brown sugar, firmly packed
1	tablespoon flour
1	teaspoon cinnamon
2	tablespoons butter or margarine
1	cup chopped pecans

To make topping, combine brown sugar, flour, and cinnamon, and mix thoroughly. Cut in butter until the consistency of cornmeal, mix in pecans and set aside. In a large mixing bowl, cream together butter and sugar. Add eggs one at a time, beating after each addition. Sift together flour, baking powder, baking soda, and salt. Add to creamed mixture alternating with sour cream, blending well after each addition. Stir in raisins.

Spread mixture in a greased 9 x 13 x 2 inch pan and sprinkle with topping. Bake at 350° (325° for glass) for 30 minutes until it tests done. Cut into squares and serve warm or cold.   **Serves 12**

A Frittata Party

A frittata is a flat, round omelet, in which herbs, vegetables or other ingredients are mixed with beaten eggs and cooked into them. Frittatas are particularly versatile. They can be eaten hot, warm or at room temperature. The ingredients can be chopped and prepared in advance. Also, once the frittata is in the oven, you can attend to preparing other delicacies. A boon to those watching their budget, ingredients for frittatas are inexpensive and readily available. Glazed with Reduced Balsamic Vinegar when taken from the pan, a frittata is a mouth-watering delight to behold and feast on.

Menu

Melon Wedge Wrapped in Prosciutto
Spinach and Roasted Pepper Frittata
Cheese Frittata with Pico de Gallo
Basket of Croissants   Bloody Marys
Sloe Gin   White Wine
Espresso   Cafe au Lait

Melon Wedges Wrapped in Prosciutto

½   *pound prosciutto ham, thinly sliced*
2   *melons*

The flavor of prosciutto, a cured ham from Italy, is a true delicacy, but if you just can't find it, choose thinly-sliced ham or turkey ham instead. Divide each slice in half lengthwise. Cut melon in half and scoop out the seeds. Quarter each piece, then slice into eighths. With a sharp paring knife, remove the rind from each wedge. Wrap one slice of ham around each wedge and secure by overlapping the edges.

Serves 16

Spinach and Roasted Pepper Frittata

½	*tablespoon light olive oil*
2	*bunches of spinach, stems removed and leaves washed*
	salt and pepper
4	*garlic cloves, finely chopped*
1	*yellow or red pepper, roasted, peeled, and diced (can also be purchased in a jar)*
2	*green onions (scallions), thinly sliced*
1/3	*cup grated parmesan cheese*
¾	*cup of crumbled feta cheese*
1	*teaspoon of finely chopped fresh rosemary*
2	*teaspoons of fresh lemon juice*
10	*eggs, beaten*
3	*tablespoons of Reduced Balsamic Vinegar*

Preheat the oven to 350°. Heat ½ tablespoon of oil in a large skillet and wilt the spinach over high heat with salt and pepper to taste. Drain and cool the spinach. Squeeze out excess moisture and coarsely chop. Place the spinach in a bowl with the remaining ingredients, except the eggs and Reduced Balsamic Vinegar. Then stir the eggs into the mixture. Pour the frittata mixture into a lightly oiled baking dish (a Pyrex pie plate works well) and bake for 25–30 minutes, until the eggs are golden and set.

Serves 8

Reduced Balsamic Vinegar

Balsamic Vinegar — the inexpensive kind, not the expensive aged vinegar.

In a small saucepan over high heat, reduce the vinegar to half its original volume. Watch carefully that all of the vinegar doesn't boil away as you reduce it.

Cheese Frittata with Pico de Gallo

Pico de Gallo

¾	*pound of ripe tomatoes, seeded and coarsely chopped, juices reserved*
1	*small jalapeno, minced*
2	*tablespoons of finely chopped fresh cilantro*
1	*teaspoon of ground cumin*
½	*teaspoon of salt*

Frittata

2	*teaspoons of unsalted butter*
10	*eggs*
½	*cup of milk*
	salt and pepper
⅓	*cup of grated Fontina cheese*
2	*tablespoons of finely chopped green onions or scallions*

Preheat the oven to 325°. In a blender or mini-processor, pulse the tomatoes, jalapeno, cilantro, and cumin until finely chopped but not pureed. Transfer to a bowl and stir in 2 tablespoons of reserved tomato juice.

Combine the eggs and milk in a medium bowl. Season to taste with salt and pepper. Pour the egg mixture into a lightly oiled baking dish. Bake until the bottom is golden and the top is still slightly runny.

Preheat the broiler. Spoon ½ cup of the pico de gallo on top of the eggs and sprinkle with cheese and scallions. Set the baking dish under the broiler until the top is set and the cheese is melted. Slide the frittata onto a large plate. Serve with the remaining pico de gallo.

Serves 8

Other Fantastic Combinations for Frittatas

- marinated artichokes, sauteed red potatoes and onions, and parmesan cheese
- caramelized onions, goat cheese, and sage
- steamed asparagus and new potatoes
- sauteed green and golden zucchini and zucchini blossoms
- steamed Yellow Finnish potatoes and lovage leaves
- wilted escarole, sauteed yellow onions, and Fontina cheese
- turkey sausage and red-skinned potatoes

Sloe Gin Fizz

Per drink:

1   *ounce Sloe Gin*
2   *ounces Sweet and Sour Mix*

Pour gin and sweet and sour mix over ice, fill glass with Club Soda.

6
A SUMPTUOUS LUNCHEON

WHETHER A SIT-DOWN or buffet, a luncheon is a festive affair characterized by light, elegantly prepared dishes enhanced by a generous assortment of breads, croissants, rolls, and muffins. The meal centers around a light main course, such as poached fish or a delicate chicken dish, and may be composed of three or four courses. When planning your menu, try to take advantage of recipes that allow dishes to be prepared well in advance and reheated or served at room temperature.

Formal Luncheon

Menu

Mushrooms Florentine   Lemon Sherbet
"Wedding" Chicken Salad   Salade Niçoise
Croissants and Sweet Butter
Double Chocolate Torte with Chantilly Cream
Champagne   White Wine   Espresso
Cafe au Lait   Tea

Mushrooms Florentine

12	*large mushrooms (2½–3" in diameter)*
2	*pounds fresh spinach or 1 (10 ounce) package frozen spinach*
3	*tablespoons butter*
1	*medium onion, minced*
1	*egg yolk*
½	*teaspoon salt*
⅛	*teaspoon pepper*
⅛	*teaspoon ground nutmeg (fresh, if possible)*
¼	*cup grated Parmesan cheese*

Preheat oven to 325°. Clean mushrooms and snap out stems. Finely chop stems and set aside. Thoroughly wash and drain spinach leaves. Cook, covered, using only the water that clings to the leaves, for 45 minutes. Squeeze out all the water from the spinach and chop finely. If using frozen spinach, be sure to drain excess water very well.

Place mushroom caps into a 8 x 6 inch baking dish. Melt butter over medium heat, add onion and mushroom stems and saute until onion is translucent. Stir in the spinach and remove pan from heat.

Combine the egg yolk, salt, pepper, nutmeg, 2½ tablespoons of Parmesan cheese and add to the spinach mixture. Stuff each individual mushroom cap with mix and sprinkle with remaining cheese. If made ahead, cover with plastic wrap and refrigerate up to 24 hours.

Bake, uncovered, for 20 minutes or until heated through and tender. Allot one or two mushrooms per person.

Serves 12

Iced Lemon Sherbet

To cleanse the palate between courses, serve a small scoop of lemon sherbet in a liqueur or small wine glass. Garnish with a sprig of fresh mint.

"Wedding" Chicken Salad

4	*cups cooked chicken breasts (skinned) cubed*
1	*cup finely chopped celery*
½	*cup finely sliced green onions*
½	*cup of chopped parsley*
2	*cups washed halved green or red seedless grapes*
1½-2	*cups mayonnaise (to taste)*
3	*teaspoons curry powder*
	salt and pepper
2	*cups cashews or peanuts (salted or unsalted)*

Mix ingredients together in large bowl. In a separate bowl, mix 1½ cups of mayonnaise with 3 teaspoons of curry powder, salt and pepper, and fold well into the salad. Arrange the mixture over leaves of romaine lettuce and raddichio.

Just before serving, add either 2 cups of cashews or 2 cups of peanuts. Serve with papaya, avocado, strawberries, and a green salad.

Serves 12–15

Find ready cooked chicken at your local butcher or delicatessen or supermarket.

Salade Niçoise

3	*pounds young green beans, steamed until tender but still crunchy*
3	*pounds red-skinned or Yukon Gold potatoes, steamed and sliced*
2	*large heads of Boston lettuce, leaves separated, rinsed, and dried*
12	*large hard-boiled eggs, cut in half lengthwise*
6–8	*ripe red tomatoes, quartered lengthwise*
3	*6-ounce cans oil-packed solid light tuna, flaked and seasoned with fresh lemon juice and freshly ground pepper.*
1oz.	*anchovy fillets packed in oil,*
4	*tablespoons capers*
½	*cup of French nicoise olives*
	chopped fresh parsley

Dressing

	grated zest of 1 lemon
	salt and freshly ground pepper
1	*tablespoon Dijon mustard*
1	*tablespoon minced shallots*
2	*tablespoons fresh lemon juice*
1	*cup good quality extra virgin olive oil*

Combine the above dressing ingredients in a screw-top jar and shake vigorously.

Shortly before serving, toss the lettuce leaves with just enough dressing to coat them. Arrange the lettuce leaves on a large platter. Pile the potatoes in the center. Place the eggs on the platter and decorate with anchovies and a few of the capers. Divide the beans, tomatoes, and tuna into portions and arrange attractively on the platter. Scatter black olives and parsley wherever needed. Serve with additional dressing on the side.

Serves 12

For a variation on the traditional Salade Niçoise, you can always substitute artichokes and ham for the tuna and anchovies. Add red and yellow peppers cut in rings, and different kinds of lettuce, such as chicory, escarole, and red-leaf romaine. It also makes a lovely presentation.

Double Chocolate Torte with Chantilly Cream

9	*ounces bittersweet chocolate*
6	*ounces sweet butter*
6	*eggs, separated*
1	*cup granulated sugar*
¼	*cup flour*
¼	*teaspoon salt*
2	*tablespoons confectioner's sugar*
1	*cup Chantilly cream*

Preheat oven to 325°. Break chocolate into small pieces and melt with the butter in a bowl over simmering water. Whip the egg yolks with ¾ cup of the granulated sugar. Gradually mix in flour, then add the melted chocolate and butter and blend well.

In a separate bowl, whip the egg whites, salt, and remaining granulated sugar to soft peaks, then fold gently into chocolate mixture.

Butter a 9 inch round cake pan and dust with flour. Pour the batter into the pan. Bake 30–40 minutes, until the center of the cake is still moist but no longer runny. Cool and turn out onto a platter.

To serve, dust the top with confectioner's sugar. Slice cake thinly and add a dollop of Chantilly cream.

Serves 8

Chantilly Cream:

1   *cup heavy cream, chilled*
1½   *teaspoons fine sugar*
½   *teaspoon vanilla extract*
     pinch of salt

Mix all the ingredients together and whip to soft peaks. Chill thoroughly.

Yields 1½ Cups

A Beautiful Buffet

A good buffet depends on variety. As you plan your menu, remember to offer a bountiful selection of salads to complement one special entree. Select dishes in an assortment of textures and colors so that your table is a feast for the eyes, as well as the palate.

Menu

Tri-Color Pasta Salad with Vegetable Medley
Ceaser Salad   Greek Salad   Waldorf Salad
Honey Dijon Chicken   Assortment of Breads
Apricot Upside-Down Cake   White Wine
Specialty Coffee   Tea

Tri-Color Pasta Salad with Vegetable Medley

1	*pound Corkscrew pasta, all white or a mixture of wheat, spinach and tomato pastas*
¾	*cup olive oil*
4	*green onions, thinly sliced*
1	*red pepper, finely chopped*
2	*large carrots, shredded coarsely*
3	*yellow squash, coarsely chopped*
1	*pound fresh broccoli, lightly steamed until just tender*
2	*tablespoons chives, minced*
1	*cup fresh basil, chopped*
1	*cup Parmesan cheese, freshly grated*
1	*tablespoon Dijon mustard*
¼	*cup balsamic vinegar*
3	*garlic cloves, minced*
1	*tablespoon sugar*
	red pepper flakes, crushed
	black pepper
	salt

Cook pasta in boiling water until al dente (firm). Drain and immediately toss with ¼ cup olive oil and cool to room temperature, stir occasionally. Add green onions, red peppers, carrots, squash, broccoli, chives, chopped basil, and ¾ cup Parmesan cheese. Mix thoroughly.

Blend together mustard, vinegar, garlic, sugar, salt and pepper, adding red pepper flakes to taste. While beating continuously, slowly add remaining olive oil. Pour over pasta and toss to mix well. Refrigerate if dish is being prepared for following day. Allow pasta to sit at room temperature for at least 2 hours before serving. Sprinkle with Parmesan cheese immediately before bringing to the table.   **Serves 12**

Caesar Salad

6–8	*heads of romaine leaves, hearts only, enough to make 20 cups of torn leaves*
4	*cloves garlic*
10	*tablespoons fruity green olive oil*
3	*tablespoons fresh-squeezed lemon juice*
2	*tablespoons Worcestershire sauce*
2	*tablespoons prepared mustard*
1–2	*tablespoons anchovy paste*
2	*tablespoons mayonnaise*
	red wine vinegar to taste
¾–1	*cup fresh-grated Reggiano Parmesan cheese*
2	*cups of croutons*
	fresh-ground black pepper

Slice one of the garlic cloves in half and use it to rub the inside of a large wooden bowl. Finely chop the remaining cloves of garlic. In a measuring cup or small glass bowl, combine the chopped garlic, mayonnaise, Worcestershire sauce, prepared mustard, anchovy paste, and lemon juice. Using a wire whisk, blend in the olive oil. Add red wine vinegar to taste and whisk the mixture again. Let stand for 15–20 minutes before using.

Wash the lettuce, spin it dry, and place in the large wooden bowl. Drizzle dressing over the lettuce and toss. Add the grated Parmesan cheese and fresh-ground pepper, and toss again. Scatter the croutons over the top, or toss them in with the lettuce.

Serves 12–18

Greek Salad

2   *large cucumbers, seeded, peeled, and sliced thin*

2   *bulbs of fennel, quartered and sliced thin*

1   *large red bell pepper, quartered and sliced thin*

1   *large yellow or orange bell pepper, quartered and sliced thin*

1   *medium red onion, thinly sliced*

2   *jars marinated artichoke hearts, well drained*

1   *cup of Mediterranean olive medley (Kalamata, cured green olives and Italian black olives)*

4–5   *tablespoons good quality fruity green olive oil*

4   *tablespoons red wine vinegar*
    few sprigs of dill

3–4   *tablespoons chopped fresh oregano*
    fresh-ground black pepper

1   *cup of crumbled feta cheese*

4   *ripe red tomatoes, cut into wedges*

Combine the cucumber, fennel, peppers, onion, artichoke hearts, and olives in a large bowl. Add olive oil and vinegar, and toss. Add dill sprigs and chopped oregano. Grind in some black pepper. Add ¾ cup of feta cheese and toss to combine. Add tomato wedges just before serving, and mix. Sprinkle the remaining feta cheese over the top.

Serves 12–16

Waldorf Salad

6   *medium red apples, cored and diced (do not peel)*

1   *cup celery, finely chopped*

½   *cup walnuts, coarsely chopped*

⅔–1   *cup mayonnaise*

In a large bowl, stir all ingredients together, adding just enough mayonnaise to ensure creamy consistency. Cover and chill 2–3 hours.

Serves 16–18

Honey Dijon Chicken

8   *chicken breasts, skinned, boned, and sliced in half*

8   *tablespoons Dijon mustard*

4   *tablespoons honey*

2   *tablespoons fresh lemon juice*

In a small bowl, mix mustard, honey, and lemon juice and blend well. Place chicken breasts in a shallow baking dish and cover with sauce. Bake, uncovered, at 350° for approximately 20 minutes, until chicken is cooked through but still moist.

Serves 16

Apricot Upside-Down Cake

4–6   *tablespoons butter*

¾   *cup brown sugar, firmly packed*

2   *(8 ounce) cans pitted apricot halves in syrup*

1   *cup all-purpose flour*

1   **teaspoon baking powder**

¼   **teaspoon salt**

3   **eggs**

1   **cup granulated sugar**

½   **gallon French vanilla ice cream**

In a heavy 10 inch frying pan with an ovenproof handle, melt butter over medium heat. Add brown sugar and cook, stirring constantly, for about 10 minutes, being careful that it doesn't burn. Drain apricots and reserve ¼ cup of the syrup. Place apricot halves, cut side up, in a single layer as close as possible to each other over brown sugar in skillet; set aside to cool.

In a small bowl, combine flour, baking powder, and salt; set aside. In another bowl, beat eggs with granulated sugar until light and fluffy, stir in ¼ cup syrup. Gently fold dry ingredients into egg mixture and pour over apricots. Bake uncovered at 350° for 35-40 minutes until toothpick inserted comes out clean. Immediately loosen cake with a spatula and invert onto serving platter.

Let skillet rest briefly on inverted cake to allow syrup to drizzle over cake. Serve warm with French vanilla ice cream. If cooked ahead of time, warm briefly in microwave or oven.

Serves 8

7
AN ELEGANT AFTERNOON TEA

INCREASINGLY POPULAR "teas" offer a luxurious way to pass an afternoon in celebration with special people. Teas can be created indoors or outdoors. Consider holding your tea shower in a lovely garden, on a lawn under umbrellas, on a patio or balcony. In or out, you'll find it a pleasure to be the hostess of a unique shower that gently speaks to the elegance and charms of earlier times. Whether you own, rent or borrow the items you'll need, this is a perfect showcase for the finest linens, china, and silver.

There are many options for tea drinking today. Black tea from India and Ceylon, such as Darjeeling and Orange Pekoe, are blended and contain caffeine. They also have a stronger, more bitter taste. Taken with milk and sugar, this is the classic English "cup-of-tea." China black tea is more delicate and should be taken plain or with lemon. You can also purchase green tea (the leaves have not been fermented as in black tea).

Green tea should be taken plain. Black teas are available with flavors added. The one preferred by many is Earl Grey, but now you can find many other flavors including Black Currant, Grapefruit, Ginger, Lemon, and Cinnamon. Decaffeinated versions of black teas and other types of fruit and herb teas are plentiful and popular, and caffeine free.

Menu

Assorted Tea Sandwiches   Genuine English Scones
Lemon Coconut Bars   Russian Tea cakes
Linzer Hearts   Walnut Bread   Shortbread Cookies
Personalized Initial Cookies   Champagne Punch
Non-alcoholic Punch   Tea

Assorted Tea Sandwiches

Purchase thinly-sliced loaves of firm white, wheat, and pumpernickel bread from a good bakery. Use a sharp knife to remove crusts, then cut the slices into assorted rectangles, triangles, and circles. Cover with plastic wrap, removing only the piece of bread you are working with. Lightly spread one side of the bread with butter or mayonnaise. Top with various fillings for open-faced sandwiches. For regular sandwiches, spread a thin layer of filling between two buttered slices of bread.

For variety, create a two-toned, layered sandwich by alternating two pieces of white with two pieces of wheat bread separated by a thin layer of cream cheese.

Egg Sandwiches

8   *thin slices of whole wheat and white bread*
    butter
¼   *cup mayonnaise*
4   *eggs*
¼   *cup parsley, finely chopped*
    salt and pepper

Boil eggs and immediately place in cold water. Shell and place in a bowl. Mash eggs with a fork and add salt and pepper. Mix in mayonnaise and parsley and blend well.

Spread butter onto a slice of bread, cover with egg mixture, and place a second slice of buttered bread on top. Cut into four pieces. Do the same with remaining slices of bread.

Makes 16 small sandwiches

Other Fine Fillings:

- *smoked turkey with cranberry sauce*
- *cream cheese with walnuts*
- *steamed baby shrimp on watercress*
- *chicken salad*
- *avocado and diced olives*
- *tuna sprinkled with dill*
- *sliced hardboiled egg and cucumber*

Breads, Cookies, and Pastries

Genuine English Scones

2   *cups flour*

¾   *stick of butter or margarine, room temperature*

1   *tablespoon of baking powder*

½   *teaspoon salt*

¼   *cup sugar*

¾   *cup whole milk*

Preheat oven to 475° To get the "real" scone look and texture, make small scones so they will rise better.

Cut the butter into the flour, stir in the sugar and salt, then take a fork and stir the milk into the mixture a little at a time. The dough should be soft and not dry.

Turn dough onto a floured board and roll to a thickness not less than ¾ inch. Cut out rings with a small fluted cookie cutter 1½ – 2 inches. Cut as many as you can and then re-knead the dough and repeat.

Place closely together on a greased cookie sheet and dust with flour. Bake 15 minutes or until golden brown. Scones should be crisp on outside and soft and fluffy on the inside. Serve warm or cold. Have plenty of butter, jam, and whipped cream on hand for guests to spread on scones.

Makes 12 scones

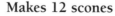 *Use buttermilk biscuit mix for your scones or buy them from your favorite bakery.*

Variations:

~ 2   teaspoons of grated orange or lemon rind

~ ½   cup currents or raisins

Lemon Bars

Crust

1½	*cups flour*
¼	*cup sugar*
1½	*sticks cold butter or margarine, cut into tiny pieces*

Topping

6	*large eggs*
3	*cups sugar*
½	*cup all-purpose flour*
2	*tablespoons freshly grated lemon peel*
1	*cup fresh lemon juice*

Preheat oven to 350°. Line an 13 x 9 inch square pan with foil and let foil extend about 2 inches above the pan on two sides. Lightly grease the foil.

For the crust, mix the flour and sugar in a bowl. Cut in the butter with a pastry blender until mixture resembles coarse crumbs. Line bottom of pan with the crust. Bake until golden, 20–25 minutes.

For the topping, beat eggs in a bowl. Add sugar, flour, lemon peel, and juice, and beat with a electric hand mixer until blended. Pour over the crust and spread evenly.

Bake until the edges are golden, about 35 minutes. Remove from the oven and cool in the pan. Lift the foil ends and place on a cutting board. Cut into 2 inch bars.

Serves 24

Russian Tea Cakes

1	cup butter, softened
½	cup confectioner's sugar
1	teaspoon vanilla
2¼	cups sifted flour
¼	teaspoon salt
¾	cup nuts, finely chopped

Preheat oven to 400°. Mix butter, sugar and vanilla, blending well. Sift together flour and salt, and add nuts. Work into nut mixture. Shape dough into 1 inch balls and place on an ungreased cookie sheet.

Bake 10–12 minutes until set but not brown. While still warm, roll in confectioner's sugar. Cool and roll in sugar once more.

Makes 4 dozen

Linzer Hearts

¾	pound sweet butter, softened
1¾	cups confectioner's sugar
1	egg
2	cups all-purpose flour, sifted
1	cup cornstarch
2	cups shelled walnuts, finely ground
½	cup red raspberry preserves

Cream butter and 1 cup sugar until light and fluffy. Add egg and mix well. Sift together the flour and cornstarch, add to creamed mixture and blend. Stir in walnuts. Gather dough into a ball, wrap in waxed paper, and chill for 4–6 hours. Roll out to ¼ inch thickness. Using a small, heart-shaped cookie cutter, cut out cookies and place on an ungreased cookie sheet. Chill for 45 minutes.

Preheat oven 325°. Bake cookies for 10–15 minutes, until evenly and lightly browned. Remove to rack to cool. While they are still slightly warm, spread half of the cookies with preserves, using ¼ teaspoon for each. Use the remaining cookies to place on top of the jam-covered bottoms. Sift remaining confectioner's sugar into a bowl and dip tops and bottoms of cookies to coat.

Makes 48

Walnut Bread

2½	*cups flour, sifted*
1	*cup sugar*
3½	*teaspoons baking powder*
1	*teaspoon salt*
3	*tablespoons vegetable oil*
1¼	*cups milk*
1	*egg*
1	*cup walnuts, finely chopped*

Grease and flour one 9 x 5 x 3 inch loaf pan or two 8½ x 4½ x 2½ inch loaf pans. In a large bowl, add all ingredients and beat until thoroughly mixed. Pour into prepared pans and bake in preheated 350° oven for 55–65 minutes. Remove from pan and cool before slicing.

Variation:

   ~ *Add one cup finely chopped dates to batter.*

Shortbread Cookies

¾   *pound sweet butter softened*
1   *cup confectioner's sugar*
3   *cups all-purpose flour, sifted*
½   *teaspoon salt*
½   *teaspoon vanilla extract*
¼   *cup granulated sugar*

Cream butter and confectioner's sugar together until light. Sift flour and salt together and add to mixture. Blend in vanilla. Form dough into ball, wrap in waxed paper, and chill for 4–6 hours. Roll out to 5/8 inch thickness. Using a 3 inch cookie cutter, cut out cookies. Sprinkle with granulated sugar and place on ungreased cookie sheets. Refrigerate for 45 minutes.

Bake in preheated oven at 325° for 20 minutes or until just starting to color lightly; cookies should not brown at all. Cool completely on wire rack.

Makes 20 cookies

Personalized Initial Cookies

1	*cup butter, softened*
½	*teaspoon salt*
1	*cup sugar*
½	*teaspoon grated lemon rind*
1½	*tablespoons lemon juice*
8	*egg yolks*
4	*cups flour, sifted*

Beat together butter and salt. Add 1 cup sugar gradually and blend until creamy. Mix in grated lemon rind and lemon juice. Beat in the egg yolks. then slowly blend in the 4 cups of flour and chill one hour. Roll the dough into sticks ¼ inch in diameter and shape into alphabet letters. Brush lightly with egg yolk and sprinkle with colored or white sugar. Bake on ungreased cookie sheet in preheated 375° oven for 6–8 minutes.

Makes 20 cookies

Champagne Punch

1	*gallon Sauterne wine*
4	*bottles champagne, one quart each*
2	*bottles ginger ale, one quart each*
½	*pint sherbet*

Chill wine, champagne, and ginger ale. Pour into large punch bowl, add sherbet and ice cubes just before serving.

Serves 40

Non-alcoholic Punch

2   *cans frozen orange juice*

2   *cans frozen lemonade*

8   *cans of cold water*

2   *cups Grenadine*

   Juice of three fresh lemons

3   *quarts ginger ale, chilled*

Mix all together in a large punch bowl right before serving. Float orange slices and cherries on the top and add ice cubes.

Serves 20

Brewing the Perfect Cup of Tea

Set up a small table or serving trolley with a pot of steaming hot water, a full pot of freshly made tea, a cream pitcher with milk, a sugar bowl filled with sugar cubes, a pair of tongs or small spoon for the sugar cubes, and a small plate of lemon circles or wedges. For an extra special touch, offer a small plate filled with clove studded lemon wedges to float in each tea cup.

Always use fresh tea bags or loose tea leaves in a tea ball. Tea, in any form, can easily pick up the flavor of where it is being stored, so it's best not to store it in a plastic container. Bring a pot of water to a rapid boil but do not let it continue to boil as this removes the air in the water and creates a tea with a flat, muddy taste. If using a tea ball, pack it with choice tea, leaving enough space for the leaves to expand slightly when wet. Warm your serving teapot with hot water and let it sit until you are ready to pour in the fresh, hot water. When making tea in a pot, the rule of thumb is to use one single tea bag or one teaspoon of loose tea per person, plus one for the pot. Teapots usually hold 4-6 cups. After emptying the pot of its warming water, pour the boiling water over the tea. Allow the tea to "blossom" by steeping for up to five minutes. Then remove the tea bags or tea ball. Prepare the table with a pitcher of whole or low fat milk, sugar cubes, a tong or small spoon, and a dish of lemon wedges studded with cloves.

Set out an assortment of tea bags and a large thermos-style carafe of hot water, and let guests prepare their own tea.

Use "multi-tasking" when it comes to opening the gifts. Have one guest help the bride-to-be unwrap her gifts and discard the paper. Ask another to make a list of who-gave-what to her and another to make the ribbon bouquet.

8

A Dessert Party

W HEN IT COMES TO DESSERTS, there's no such thing as too many, so go ahead and plan a party that will be sweetly sensational! Centering your shower around these luscious treats allows you to spoil your guests by combining two not-to-be-missed luxuries — good friends and sweet desserts.

Menu

Blueberry Cream Cheese Tart   *Apricot Upside-Down Cake*
Chocolate Coconut Bars   *Double Chocolate Torte*
English Trifle   *Amaretto Mousse*
Fresh Strawberries Dipped in Chocolate
Champagne   *Cafe Especial*

Blueberry Cream Cheese Tart

4   *ounces natural cream cheese*
¼   *cup sour cream*
1–2   *teaspoons sugar*

3   *cups blueberries*
¼ *cup sugar nutmeg*
   grated peel of one lemon
   powdered sugar
   tart dough

Tart Crust

1   *cup all-purpose flour*
    pinch salt
1   *tablespoon sugar*
¼ *teaspoon grated orange peel*
4   *ounces unsalted butter, room temperature*
1   *tablespoon water*
½ *teaspoon vanilla*

Combine the flour, salt, sugar, and orange peel in a bowl. Cut the butter into small pieces, then cut in dry ingredients, using two knives or a pastry cutter, to make a coarse meal. Combine water and vanilla and stir into mixture with a fork. Gather dough into a ball and flatten into a round disc, wrap in plastic, and place in the refrigerator for ½ hour.

Line a 9 inch tart pan with dough, shaping the sides first. Using your hands, shape sides of uniform thickness, forming an edge that rises about ¼ inch above the rim of the pan. Press dough gently into bottom of pan and place in freezer for 30 minutes. Prick bottom of tart with a fork and bake at 400° for 15 minutes until golden brown. Set aside to cool.

Cream Cheese Filling

Beat together the cream cheese, sour cream, and lemon until they are well combined. Add 1–2 teaspoons sugar and a pinch of nutmeg.

Heat ½ cup berries in a saucepan. As soon as they begin to release their juices, add ¼ cup sugar and continue cooking until smooth and syrupy (about 12 minutes). Pour cooked fruit over rest of berries and gently mix.

To assemble, spread cream cheese mixture evenly over crust and top with berries. Dust edges with powdered sugar. Remove tart carefully from its ring and set on a flat serving plate. Cut into wedges for serving.

Serves 6–8

Apricot Upside-Down Cake

(See Page 72)

Chocolate Coconut Bars

½	*cup butter*
1½	*cups graham cracker crumbs*
1	*14-ounce can sweetened condensed milk (not evaporated milk)*
1	*6-ounce package semisweet chocolate chips*
1	*cup walnuts, chopped*
1	*3½ ounce can flaked coconut*

Preheat oven to 350° (325° for glass dish). Melt butter in a 13 x 9 inch baking pan by placing briefly in oven. Sprinkle crumbs over butter, mix, and press firmly into bottom of pan. Pour condensed milk evenly over crumbs and top with chocolate chips, walnuts, and flaked coconut; press down firmly.

Bake 25–30 minutes or until lightly browned. Cool thoroughly before cutting.

Makes 24 bars

For a quick, low-fat dessert idea you might think about blending up a few refreshing fruit smoothies. Serve them in tall, see-through glasses with sprigs of fresh herbs for a winning effect.

Double Chocolate Torte

(See Page 67)

English Trifle

2	*cups of sliced cake (pound cake, lemon bread, or sponge cake)*
	raspberry or strawberry jam
8	*ounces of frozen raspberries or strawberries (do not defrost)*
½–1	*cup sherry*
2	*bananas peeled and sliced thinly*
¼	*cup lemon juice*
8	*ounces of whipping cream, whipped to stiff peaks*
½	*cup sliced almonds*

Custard

2	cups whole milk
4	egg yolks
½	sugar
1	teaspoon of cornstarch
½	teaspoon of vanilla

Lay the cake on the bottom of a large glass bowl. Pour the sherry over the cake and let it soak in (the cake should be moist). Use orange juice if you want an alcohol-free version. Spread with jam. Add the frozen raspberries or strawberries.

Make the custard by heating the milk slowly in a small saucepan. Mix the egg yolks, sugar, cornstarch, and vanilla in a bowl. When the cream is hot pour it over the egg mixture, stirring constantly. Return the mixture to the saucepan and heat until thick.

Allow it to cool and then sprinkle the bananas over the raspberries or strawberries and pour on the custard.

Chill for 3–4 hours. Just before serving, spread whipped cream over the top and sprinkle with almonds.

Serves 12

If you're making English trifle, look for imported English custard powder at your supermarket. It's instant — just add milk and sugar or use your favorite pudding mix

Amaretto Mousse

4	*tablespoons sweet butter*
5	*eggs*
1	*cup granulated sugar*
1½	*teaspoons unflavored gelatin*
¾	*cup tiny macaroons (amaretti), crushed*
1½	*tablespoons Amaretto liqueur*
1½	*cups heavy cream, chilled*

Melt butter in top half of a double boiler over simmering water. Beat eggs with sugar; add gelatin. Stir into melted butter and cook, stirring continuously, until thickened (6–8 minutes.) Remove from heat. Mix in the Amaretto and crushed macaroons, blending thoroughly. Cool and place in refrigerator until mixture just begins to set.

Whip cream to soft peaks and gently fold into Amaretto mixture. Spoon into individual wine goblets or a large glass serving bowl. Chill until set, approximately 4 hours. Sprinkle with crushed macaroons and serve.

Serves 8–10

Fresh Strawberries Dipped in Chocolate

24	*Fresh large strawberries, rinsed with stems left intact*
12	*ounces semi-sweet or milk chocolate pieces*
¾	*cup light cream*
12	*tablespoons Kirsch, Cointreau, brandy, or 2 teaspoons coffee*

In a heavy saucepan, melt chocolate and cream over low heat, stirring until smooth. Remove from heat and blend in liqueur. Holding each berry by the stem, swirl in chocolate to partially cover and lay on waxed paper to dry. Once chocolate is hardened, arrange fruit on a silver platter. For a lively buffet table, give guests the option of dipping their own strawberries. Pour chocolate sauce into a fondue pot or chafing dish to keep warm, and place berries in a bowl for the guests to help themselves to this delightful treat.

Makes 24

Cafe Especial

With the rise of coffee bars across the country, it's easy to find fresh specialty coffee beans at your local cafés and supermarkets. You can have them ground in the store or take them home and grind them yourself. You might even consider inventing your own blend by combining two special flavors — mix Viennese Roast with Vanilla Bean, for instance. Try out a few possible combinations before deciding on the final one to serve.

Keep the coffee piping hot in a large thermal carafe or in a pot placed on a warming plate. Avoid letting the coffee sit too long so that it doesn't become bitter. One secret to great-tasting coffee is a clean machine. If you own either a steam- or a pump-driven machine for making espresso and cappuccino, you might consider making cappuccinos and lattes for your guests.

Stock your coffee table with a pitcher of cream, a container of hot milk, a bowl of whipped cream, a bowl of sugar cubes and tongs, and for that special touch, a dish of chocolate chips and a saucer of cinnamon sticks.

It's also a good idea to have a pot of decaffeinated coffee. Don't forget the artificial sweetener and non-dairy creamer for those with special tastes. Display them nicely in attractive containers.

A dessert shower is perfect for the office at the end of the day. Have your local bakery deliver the goodies directly to you. Grab a few cartons of ice cream at the deli — along with a few toppings — and you're set for a delectable celebration. Colorful paper plates with coordinating napkins and some helium balloons add the icing on the cake!

9
COCKTAILS AND
HORS D'OEUVRES

ODAY'S "GRAZING" TASTES allow for substantial hors
d'oeuvres to serve as a meal. If accompanies by a basket of
specialty breads and crackers (French, Italian, Sour Dough, etc.)
your guests will be able to put together a delicious plate of treats.

Classic Cocktail Party

Menu

Stuffed Snow Peas　　*Savory Artichoke Dip*
Mushrooms Stuffed with Sweet Sausage
Everyone's Favorite Spinach Dip
Crab-filled Cherry Tomatoes
Shrimp in Prosciutto
Chicken Satés　　*Sweet-and-Sour Meatballs*
Cheese and Pâte Platter
Open Bar

Stuffed Snow Peas

48   snow peas
 8   ounces cream cheese, at room temperature
 ¼   cup fresh parsley, chopped
 ¼   cup fresh dill, chopped
 1   garlic clove, minced
      black pepper (optional)

In salted, boiling water, blanch snow peas for 30 seconds. Cool in cold water, drain and set aside. Blend the rest of the ingredients until smooth. With a sharp pan knife, split the snow peas open along the curved side. Fill each with filling, using a small spatula or pastry bag with tip. Can be made the day before, refrigerate, and serve chilled.

Savory Artichoke Dip

2   6-ounce jars artichoke hearts, drained
1   cup mayonnaise
1   cup Parmesan cheese
1   medium size onion

Preheat oven to 350°. Blend together artichoke hearts, mayonnaise, Parmesan cheese, and onion, in an electric blender until smooth and creamy. Pour into shallow baking dish and bake for 30 minutes. Serve warm with small crackers.

Serves 12

Mushrooms Stuffed with Sweet Sausage

1   *tablespoon olive oil plus additional for brushing the mushroom caps*

2   *sweet Italian sausages*

¹/₃ *cup minced garlic*

¹/₃ *cup minced onion*

1   *garlic clove, minced*

1   *pound (about 14) large mushrooms, stems removed and chopped fine*

2   *tablespoons medium-dry sherry*

½   *cup coarse fresh bread crumbs, toasted lightly*

1   *large egg yolk beaten lightly*

2   *tablespoons minced fresh parsley leaves*

Heat 1 tablespoon of the oil over moderate heat and sauté sausage for 1 minute. Add onion .Cook until onion is soft and sausage is done. Add the garlic, and cook for 1 minute. Add the mushroom stems and salt and pepper to taste and cook the mixture until the liquid the mushrooms give off is evaporated. Remove skillet from heat and stir in bread crumbs. Let the mixture cool and blend in the egg yolk, parsley, and salt and pepper to taste.

Brush the outside of each mushroom cap with some of the oil. Divide the filling among the caps. Arrange the stuffed mushrooms in a lightly oiled baking dish, just large enough to hold them in one layer. Bake in a preheated 400° oven for 5–10 minutes, or until they are golden.

Variation:

Use the Spanish chorizo sausage or 1/3 cup of pepperoni for a spicy

Everyone's Favorite Spinach Dip

1	*package fresh or frozen spinach, chopped*
1	*cup mayonnaise*
16	*ounces sour cream*
1	*package dried vegetable soup and recipe mix*
8	*ounces water chestnuts, drained and chopped*
4	*scallions, finely chopped*

Let frozen spinach thaw and drain it well or place fresh spinach in a pan with about ½ inch of water and bring to a quick boil. Cook for about 2 minutes until the spinach has wilted. Drain well and chop with a pair of scissors.

Mix spinach and rest of ingredients in a bowl until well blended. Cover and refrigerate for 2 hours or longer. Serve with Italian, French or pita bread.

Crab-filled Cherry Tomatoes

Hollow out 36 cherry tomatoes and drain upside down on paper towels. Slice a thin piece off the bottom of each tomato so that it will sit in place on serving tray.

Crab Cream Filling:

1	*cup crab meat, shredded*
¼	*cup fresh lime juice*
3	*ounces cream cheese, softened*
¼	*cup cream*
2	*tablespoons mayonnaise*
1	*tablespoon onions, minced*

½   *teaspoon garlic, minced*

1   *teaspoon dried dill*

1   *teaspoon Worcestershire sauce*

2   *drops Tabasco sauce*

    salt to taste

Marinate crab meat in lime juice for 1 hour and drain well. Combine cream cheese, cream, and mayonnaise until smooth. Add to drained crab meat, blend in remaining ingredients, and mix well. Fill individual tomatoes and chill until serving time.

Shrimp in Prosciutto

40   *shrimp*

½   *pound prosciutto, thinly sliced*

2   *tablespoons sweet rice wine vinegar*

2   *tablespoons champagne vinegar*

½   *cup olive oil*

2   *garlic cloves, crushed*

Cook shrimp in boiling water 2–3 minutes until done. Drain, cool in cold water, drain again, and set aside in glass bowl. Mix vinegars, oil, and garlic. Pour over shrimp, stirring to coat thoroughly. Refrigerate overnight.

To serve, wrap each shrimp in a narrow piece of prosciutto, overlapping edges to hold in place.

Chicken Satés

3   *pounds boneless chicken breast, cut in ¾" cubes*

1   *medium onion, minced*

1   *large fresh hot chili, seeded and chopped*
3   *teaspoons ginger root, minced*
3   *tablespoons lime juice*
1   *tablespoon salt*
2   *tablespoons soy sauce*
2   *tablespoons vegetable oil*

In a large glass bowl, combine everything except poultry and blend well. Add chicken pieces and allow to marinate overnight in refrigerator.

Remove chicken from marinade and place on bamboo skewers, allotting two pieces per skewer. Place in shallow baking dish and pour remaining marinade over chicken. Place under broiler until cooked through. Serve warm with sauce for dipping.

Dipping Sauce
1   *cup sherry*
¼   *cup brown sugar*
4   *tablespoons soy sauce*
3   *tablespoons rice wine vinegar*
3   *scallions, chopped*

Combine sherry, sugar, soy sauce, and vinegar in a small saucepan. Cook over medium heat for 20 minutes, remove and add the scallions. Serve at room temperature.

Sweet-and-Sour Meatballs

1½	*pound lean ground beef*
1	*egg*
2	*tablespoons flour*
½	*teaspoon salt*
¼	*teaspoon ground black pepper*
½	*cup peanut oil*
1	*cup chicken broth*
2	*large green peppers, diced*
1	*8-ounce can pineapple chunks*
3	*tablespoons cornstarch*
1	*teaspoon soy sauce*
½	*cup pineapple juice*
½	*cup vinegar*
½	*cup sugar*

Shape meat into small balls. Mix egg, flour, salt, and pepper into a smooth batter. Heat peanut oil in large skillet. Dip meat balls in batter and fry until brown. Remove and keep warm. Pour off all but one tablespoon of oil and add ½ cup chicken broth, green pepper, and pineapple. Blend remaining ingredients and add to skillet. Cook, stirring constantly, until mixture comes to a boil and thickens. Return meatballs to sauce and heat through. Spear each meatball with a toothpick for easy serving and arrange in chafing dish.

Cheese and Pâte Platter

Purchase two types of cheese and one nice pâte. Serve with a selection of whole-grain crackers or thin slices of French bread.

A Tapas Celebration

The tradition of the Spaniards to meander from bar to bar to meet and share appetizers with family and friends can be easily transformed into a delightful shower occasion. With tapas, almost any Spanish wine will do well. Choose from a variety of Riojas, whites, rosés, and sparkling wines.

Menu

Frittata   Marinated Baby Artichokes
Anchovies Tapenade
Garlic Shrimp
Balsamic Bell Peppers   Stuffed Eggs
Crab Cakes   Spanish Herbed Patatas   Grilled Chorizo
Spanish Wines and Sherries
Sangria

Frittata

(See recipes on Pages 60, 61 and 62)

Marinated Baby Artichokes

2	*cups champagne vinegar*
8	*fresh bay leaves*
2	*teaspoons salt*
16	*baby artichokes*
4	*garlic cloves, cut in half*
2	*tablespoons minced fresh flat leaf parsley*
1½	*cups olive oil*

In a large nonreactive saucepan combine 2 cups of water with the vinegar, 4 of the bay leaves and the salt.

Trim the artichokes by removing the tough outer leaves and cutting the stem close to the base. Using a very sharp knife, chop off about ½ inch of the top center leaves. Then, using scissors, clip the remaining thorny leaves. To keep the artichoke from turning brown, drop it immediately into the vinegar mixture after cutting.

Bring the artichokes and the liquid to a simmer and cook until tender, about 8 minutes.

While the artichokes are still warm, layer them in a glass container with garlic, parsley, and the remaining bay leaves. Pour in enough of the oil to cover the artichokes completely and set aside to cool. Cover tightly and refrigerate for at least 24 hours before serving.

Serves 16

A wine and cheese party sets the tempo for a fast and simple, yet exceptional, affair. When the right cheese meets the right wine, the result is a sensational marriage. Sauvignon Blanc and goat cheese is a marriage made in heaven. A classic cheese fondue as your centerpiece will "wow" your guests into a sublime state.

Anchovies Tapenade

1 *pound dry, oil-cured black olives, pitted*
2 *2-ounce cans anchovy fillets, drained and rinsed with cold water*
2 *teaspoons capers*
   black pepper
1 *clove garlic, peeled*
3 *tablespoons extra virgin olive oil*
4 *ounces canned tuna, drained*

Combine all the ingredients in a food processor and process until well blended. Serve on toasted rounds of a French or Italian baguette.

Serves 12–14

Garlic Shrimp

1½ *cups olive oil*
 8 *medium garlic cloves, sliced thin*
 3 *pounds medium shrimp, shelled and devined*
    dried red pepper flakes
 2 *tablespoons minced fresh parsley, flat leaf*
    juice from 1 lemon
    salt
    French baguettes

In a heavy skillet, combine the oil and the garlic and cook over moderate heat, stirring occasionally with a wooden spoon until the garlic begins to turn golden, about 1 minute. Add the shrimp and dried red pepper flakes to taste. Cook until the shrimp are opaque throughout.

Remove the skillet from the heat. Add parsley, lemon juice, and salt to taste. Serve on small plates with plenty of bread to soak up the juice.

Serves 16–20

Balsamic Bell Peppers

12   *red and/or yellow bell peppers, cored, seeded, and quartered lengthwise*

1   *cup balsamic vinegar*

½   *cup extra-virgin olive oil*

   salt

Place the peppers in a skillet and toss with the vinegar and a teaspoon of salt. Cover and cook over low heat, stirring occasionally with a wooden spoon, until tender, about 30 minutes.

With a slotted spoon, transfer the peppers to a large platter. Beat the oil into the skillet with the vinegar until the mixture is warmed through. Pour the liquid over the peppers, season with additional salt to taste, and let cool for 30 minutes before serving.

Serves 12-14

Stuffed Eggs

12   *hardboiled eggs*

   mayonnaise

   handful of green pimento olives, chopped

2   *tablespoons of capers*

1   *tablespoon anchovy paste*

   olive oil

   paprika

To hard boil eggs:

I learned this from Julia Child. It's the best method of hard boiling eggs I've come across. With a pushpin, pierce the large end of each egg to release the air bubble. Place the eggs in a large saucepan and pour in enough cold water to cover the eggs completely. Bring just to the boil, remove from the heat, put a lid on the saucepan and let the eggs stand for 17 minutes. Transfer the eggs to a bowl of ice cold water. Bring the cooking water back to the boil. Immerse the eggs in the rapidly boiling water for 10 seconds. Peel the eggs under cold running water.

To stuff the eggs:

Cut each egg in half and remove the yolks. Mix yolks with chopped olives, capers, anchovy paste, mayonnaise and a dash of olive oil. Stuff egg halves, sprinkle with paprika and serve chilled.

Serves 24

Crab Cakes

1	*pound crabmeat*
10	*ounces Yukon Gold potatoes*
2	*tablespoons capers*
2	*tablespoons fresh lime juice*
2	*teaspoons lime zest*
4	*scallions, finely chopped (white and green parts)*
	pinch cayenne
2	*tablespoons chopped fresh parsley*
	salt and pepper
	vegetable oil for frying

Put unpeeled potatoes in a saucepan with boiling water and salt and simmer for 10 minutes. Drain and set aside to cool. Meanwhile, mix together the rest of the ingredients in a mixing bowl. Peel the cooled potatoes and grate them on the coarse side of a grater. Combine with the crab mixture. Then take a heaping tablespoon of the mixture and form into a little cake. Carefully place each cake on a large baking sheet. When all the cakes are made, cover them with plastic food wrap and chill in the refrigerator for 2 hours.

To cook, heat 3 tablespoons of oil in a heavy frying pan, making sure it is very hot, then gently slide in the crab cakes using a spatula. Cook them for 3 minutes on each side. Remove them to a plate lined with paper towels to drain, then transfer to a warmed serving platter and garnish with lime quarters and parsley.

Serves 8–10

Spanish Herbed Patatas

4   *russet potatoes, peeled*
¼   *cup olive oil*
2   *teaspoons minced garlic*
3   *tablespoons of fresh herbs (parsley, rosemary, and thyme)*
     salt and pepper

Preheat oven to 425°. Cut potatoes lengthwise into ½ inch thick sticks. In a baking pan, mix potato sticks, garlic, herbs, and oil. Arrange potatoes slightly apart in a single layer. Bake for 30 minutes or until potatoes are well browned. Turn them occasionally. Transfer to a platter. Add salt and pepper to taste.

Serves 12

Grilled Chorizo Sausage

6   *links of chorizo or other spicy sausage*

Grill or broil sausage for 20 minutes and cut into ¼ inch diagonal slices. Serve with toothpicks.

Serves 12–14

Sangria

1   *lemon*

1   *large apple*

2   *bottles dry red wine*

24   *ounces club soda, chilled*

1   *orange*

½   *cup sugar, or to taste*

½   *cup brandy*

Slice lemon and orange into ¼ inch slices; core apple, cut in half and then cut into thin slices. Combine fruit and sugar in a large pitcher. Add wine and brandy and stir. Chill in refrigerator. Just before serving, add the club soda. Stir and serve in chilled wine goblets or over ice.

Serves 24

A table full of tapas, in the Spanish tradition, can be a wonderful time-saver. There are many buy-and-serve options. Choose from a wide array of foods, from Spanish-style olives to marinated clams. Sliced tomatoes drizzled with olive oil and garnished with capers, marinated anchovies, grilled chorizo sausage and cheese wedges are all quick and easy additions. Be sure to have plenty of baguette slices on hand.

10
GALA DINNERS

*E*VENING FARE for a bridal shower includes exquisite buffets, tostada bars, backyard barbeques, elegant sit-down dinners, informal pasta parties, and many other types of festivities evoked by your imagination. If you choose a buffet-style celebration, it helps to select dishes that can be served cool or at room temperature. Much of this food can be prepared in advance, not to mention that the true flavors of food are best appreciated at these temperatures. If you have a favorite recipe that must be served heated, be sure to keep it warm in a chafing dish.

A Buffet Party

Menu

Savory Artichoke Dip   *Cheese and Pâte Platter*
Tri-Colored Pasta Salad with Vegetable Medley
Roasted Chicken with Black Olives and Sausage
Foil-Baked Fresh Whole Salmon   *Spinach Salad*
Rosti Broccoli with Olive Sauce   *French Bread*
Mocha Charlotte   *White Wine*   *Coffee*

Savory Artichoke Dip

(See Page 96)

Cheese and Pâte Platter

There are hundreds, if not thousands, of cheeses on the market today. They range from mild to strong. Pâtes are plentiful as well, so you don't have to make your own. There are even some delicious vegetable pâtes available. For the most pleasing platter, choose an assortment of soft, semi-soft and hard cheeses that complement your choice of pâtes. For color, add rings of red and yellow bell pepper and sprigs of fresh herbs tied together with cord.

Tri-Color Pasta Salad with Vegetable Medley

(See Page 69)

Roasted Chicken with Black Olives and Sausage

3	*2½-pound frying chickens, cut into serving pieces*
6	*cloves garlic*
6	*tablespoons olive oil*
	juice of 1 lemon, or more to taste
1	*bunch fresh rosemary, coarsely chopped*
2	*pounds sweet Italian sausage, or other non-pork variety*
1	*cup pitted Nicoise olives*
10–12	*plum tomatoes, cut lengthwise into wedges (or one can plum tomatoes, chopped coarse)*
3	*tablespoons butter*

4   *tablespoons grated Parmesan cheese*
½   *cup red wine*

Preheat oven to 375°. Smash 3 of the garlic cloves and rub them over the chicken pieces. Sprinkle with 3 tablespoons of olive oil, the lemon juice, salt, pepper, and half the rosemary. Place the chicken in an ungreased baking pan and bake for 45 minutes, or until the juice runs clear. Transfer to a buffet warmer.

Meanwhile, sauté sausage in a separate skillet in 2 tablespoons of olive oil for 15–20 minutes. Remove the skin and cut into ½ inch pieces. Set aside. Smash the remaining cloves of garlic and put them in the pan. Add remaining olive oil and cook the garlic until it begins to brown. Add the tomatoes and remaining rosemary. Sprinkle with salt and pepper to taste. Sauté until the tomatoes begin to soften. Stir in the wine. Add the butter and Parmesan cheese and stir briskly until the sauce becomes smooth and creamy. Pour sauce over chicken. Keep warm in a chafing dish.

Serves 10–12

Foil-Baked Fresh Whole Salmon

1   *whole fresh salmon (1–1½ pounds*
2   *or more ounces of butter*
2   *bay leaves*
    salt and pepper

Preheat oven to 250°. Wipe the fish with paper towels, then place it in the center of a large double sheet of generously-buttered foil. Place butter and bay leaves in the cavity of the fish, and spread more of the butter on top. Season well with salt and pepper. Wrap the foil over the salmon, place on a heatproof plate, and bake in the oven for 1 hour. When cool carefully remove the skin and serve on a bed of lettuce.

Rosti Broccoli with Olive Sauce

½	*pound butter or margarine*
1	*cup slivered almonds, lightly toasted*
6	*tablespoons lemon juice*
2	*garlic cloves, crushed*
1	*(4 ½ ounces) can sliced ripe olives, drained*
5–6	*pounds firm fresh broccoli, separated into small florets with 1-inch stems*
2	*tablespoons oil*

To make sauce:

Melt butter or margarine in a small skillet. Add almonds, lemon juice, garlic, and olives. Let stand 1 hour so flavors will blend. Reheat before serving.

To prepare broccoli:

Blanch the broccoli in boiling salted water for about 1 minute. Drain and pour cold water over it. Dry on paper towels.

Heat the broiler. Place broccoli florets on their sides on a broiler rack and season with salt and pepper; sprinkle with oil. Cook until lightly charred, turning once. Arrange florets on a large platter and and ladle sauce over it.

Serves 16

Spinach Salad with Lemon Dressing

3   *bags pre-washed baby spinach leaves*
2   *hard boiled eggs, chopped*
6   *slices bacon, cooked and crumbled*
1   *red onion, sliced thin*
¼   *cup fresh lemon juice*
½   *cup extra virgin olive oil*
    salt and pepper

Place spinach leaves in a large wooden salad bowl. Sprinkle chopped eggs and crumbled bacon on top. Whisk together lemon juice and olive oil. Season with salt and pepper. Just before serving, pour over spinach and toss thoroughly. Garnish with red onion slices.

Serves 10–12

Mocha Charlotte

1   *pound semi-sweet baking chocolate*
6   *egg yolks*
6   *egg whites*
½   *cup sugar*
3   *tablespoons instant coffee*
½   *cup boiling water*
1½   *cups heavy cream, whipped*
1   *teaspoon vanilla*
½   *cup heavy cream*
     chocolate shavings

Melt chocolate over simmering water. Let ½ cup water come to a boil, add coffee, stir to dissolve and allow to cool slightly.

In a medium-sized bowl, beat egg yolks at high speed until foamy. Gradually add sugar, beating continuously until mixture is quite thick and pale yellow. Reduce speed and mix in coffee, vanilla, and melted chocolate.

With clean beaters, beat egg whites in a large bowl until they hold stiff peaks. Blend 1 cup of the beaten whites into chocolate mixture, then stir all of the chocolate into the remaining whites. Gently fold in whipped cream, stirring to thoroughly blend. Line a 9 inch springform pan with 24 Lady Fingers, split and brushed with ¼ cup light rum. Overlap bottom pieces to fit pan snugly. Pour in batter and freeze up to one month.

To serve, remove from freezer 20–25 minutes before needed and remove springform sides. Whip ½ cup heavy cream and pile on top of the charlotte. Add chocolate shavings to garnish.

Serves 8–10

Tostada Bar

Menu

Tortilla Chips   Chili and Cheese Dip   Guacamole
Bean Dip   Chicken Olé   Tasty Tostadas
Tropical Banana Salsa   Mango Salsa
Flan   Margaritas   Beer
Mexican Coffee

Chili and Cheese Dip

2   *tablespoons vegetable oil*
1   *cup onions, chopped*

2   *small garlic cloves, minced*

1   *4-ounce can chopped green chilies*

2   *jalapeno chilies, roasted, peeled, and chopped*

1   *8-ounce can stewed tomatoes*

2   *cups Monterey Jack cheese, shredded*

2   *cups Cheddar cheese, shredded*

1   *cup sour cream*

In a large saucepan, heat oil and add garlic and onions. Cook until tender but not brown. Add chilies and tomatoes, breaking up the larger pieces. Lower heat and stir in cheeses, cooking until melted. Blend in sour cream, cook until heated through but do not allow to come to a boil.

Makes 4 Cups

Guacamole

4   *medium avocados*

2   *small tomatoes, chopped*

4   *tablespoons onion, minced*

2   *teaspoons lemon juice*

1   *teaspoon garlic powder*

1   *teaspoon salt*

Peel avocados, cut in half lengthwise, and discard the pit. In a large bowl, mash the avocados with a fork until smooth. Stir in tomatoes, onion, lemon juice, garlic powder, and salt. Serve immediately.

Serves 12–14

Bean Dip

1   *16-ounce can refried beans*
1   *4-ounce can green chilies, diced*
1   *7-ounce can Ortega chili salsa*
1   *package taco seasoning*
8   *ounces whipped cream cheese*
1   *pound Cheddar cheese, grated*

In a large bowl, mix together beans, chilies, salsa, taco seasoning, and cream cheese. Stir in three fourths of the grated cheese and pour mixture into a 9 x 13 x 2 inch baking dish. Sprinkle with remaining cheese and bake at 350° for 30 minutes. For serving, keep dip warm in chafing dish or on a hot plate.

Makes 4 cups

Chicken Olé

5   *chicken breasts*
1   *dozen corn tortillas, cut into I" strips*
1   *medium onion, diced*
3   *cups Cheddar cheese, grated*
1   *can cream of chicken soup*
1   *can cream of mushroom soup*
1   *cup milk*
1   *7-ounce can red chili salsa*

Boil chicken breasts until cooked, remove skin and bones. Tear into bite-sized pieces and set aside.

Combine soups, milk, and salsa, mixing until smooth. In a large casserole dish, spread a thin coating of sauce followed by a layer of tortilla strips, a layer of chicken pieces, a covering of cheese, and a layer of onions. Continue layering in this manner, finishing with a layer of sauce. Sprinkle the top with cheese. Cover and bake at 325° for 1 hour. Remove cover and bake an additional 30 minutes.

Serves 10–12

Tasty Tostadas

2 *dozen corn tortillas*

1 *16 ounce can refried beans, heated*

3 *pounds lean ground beef, crumbled and fried*

3 *cups cooked and shredded chicken breast*

1 *large bead of lettuce, finely shredded*

3 *cups Cheddar cheese, grated*

3 *cups tomatoes, chopped*

2 *cups sour cream*

1 *cup green onions, including tops, diced*

3 *cups guacamole*

2 *cups salsa*

   oil for frying

Pour oil ¼ inch deep into a medium skillet. Fry each tortilla in the hot oil until brown and crisp. Remove and drain on paper towels. Set aside until needed for party.

To serve, arrange all tostada components in a row and allow each guest to assemble her own tostada. Stack tortillas at beginning of assembly line. Place separate bowls of the following ingredients in the order that they are needed: refried beans, ground beef, chicken, lettuce, cheese, tomatoes, sour cream, green onions, guacamole, and salsa. If you are planning on having quite a few guests, arrange the ingredients in two separate rows on both ends of the buffet table.

Serves 12

Tropical Banana Salsa

2   *bananas, diced*
2   *tomatoes, peeled seeded and diced*
1   *tablespoon scallions, diced*
1   *teaspoon sesame seeds*
2   *teaspoons fresh lemon juice*
     salt and pepper to taste

Mix all ingredients together in a bowl.

Makes 2 cups

Mango Salsa

1   *cup fresh corn (may substitute frozen)*
1   *cup ripe mango, chopped*
1   *cup jicama, chopped*
1   *small red onion, chopped*
½   *cup cilantro, chopped*
1   *clove garlic, crushed*

Thaw corn if using frozen. Mix together all ingredients in a small bowl and chill in refrigerator for 1 hour.

Makes 3 cups

Flan

¾   cup sugar

1   *14-ounce can sweetened condensed milk*

1   *cup whipping cream*

½   *cup milk*

4   *eggs*

1   *cinnamon stick*

Melt sugar in a 7 inch saucepan over medium heat. Reduce heat and continue to cook, stirring occasionally. When sugar is melted and brown, immediately spoon over bottom and sides of a shallow 1½ quart baking dish. Set aside while caramel cools in dish. Preheat oven to 325°.

Combine condensed milk, cream, milk, and eggs, in blender and mix thoroughly. Pour into baking dish with caramelized sugar and drop a whole cinnamon stick into the middle of the mixture.

Position baking dish inside larger pan filled with hot water. Water should reach halfway up sides of baking dish. Bake 1 hour and 50 minutes or until a knife comes out clean when inserted. Check during baking in case flan is browning too quickly. If so, cover loosely with foil.

When done, cool and refrigerate at least 3 hours. To serve, run a knife around edges and invert carefully onto serving plate.

Serves 8–10

Margaritas

1¼	cups freshly squeezed lime juice
1	cup tequila
⅓	cup Cointreau
⅓	cup sugar (or more, if needed)
	lime wedges
	coarse salt
	ice cubes

Rub the rims of stemmed goblets with lime wedges. Dip the rims into a saucer filled with salt to coat edges of glasses.

Fill a blender three-fourths full with ice cubes. Pour in lime juice, tequila, and Cointreau, add sugar, and blend. Mix at high speed until mixture is frothy. Taste and add more sugar, if needed. Pour into prepared glasses and serve immediately.

Makes 45 drinks

If you would like to create a special dinner and you have a limited amount of time, you might want to try using some of the pre-packaged salad, soup, and sauce mixes for Indian or Thai "curry in a hurry." There are many available in stores today. Follow the directions on the package. Add fresh condiments to the table, such as coconut, bananas, tomatoes, and cucumbers and chopped mint in plain yogurt. You'll also find some irresistible buy-and-serve chutneys in your local supermarkets.

Mexican Coffee

1 *ounce Kahlua*
½ *ounce brandy*
1 *teaspoon chocolate syrup*
hot coffee
dash cinnamon
sweetened whipped cream

Place Kahlua, brandy, chocolate syrup, and cinnamon in coffee cup or mug. Fill with hot coffee and stir to blend. Top with whipped cream and serve immediately.

Makes 1 drink

I make a quick and delicious salsa by adding the following to my favorite commercial brand: *16-ounce can of chopped tomatoes, fresh lime juice, finely chopped scallions, finely chopped cucumber, and lots of chopped cilantro.*

Pasta Party

Menu

Antipasto   Angel Hair Pasta with Pesto
Lemon Pasta with Salmon   Tagliatelli Primavera
Italian Sausage Lasagna   Garlic Bread
Blueberry and Peach Tartlets
Italian Red and White Wines

Antipasto

Antipasto is a lavish arrangement of meats, cheeses, vegetables, and condiments. In recreating this Italian delicacy, have condiments cut in bite-sized pieces and meats and cheeses thinly sliced. After slicing, roll meat slices and place seamed side down on platters. Cheese should be sliced in diagonal strips before rolling. Arrange on platter with meat and fill in with marinated mushrooms, peppers, olives, artichoke hearts, and whatever else suits your fancy.

Go to your local Italian or specialty market to find the following antipasto ingredients:

Mozzarella	*Mascarpone*
Provolone	*pepperoni*
salami	*prosciutto*
Capicola	*hot peppers*
roasted red peppers	*marinated mushrooms*
marinated hearts of palm	*marinated artichoke hearts*
marinated olives	

Angel Hair Pasta with Pesto

4	*pounds angel hair pasta, cooked al dente and drained*
½	*pound whole pine nuts*
½	*cup pignoli nuts*
4	*garlic cloves, peeled*
1	*teaspoon salt*
½	*teaspoon ground pepper*
3–4	*cups fresh basil leaves*
¼	*pound freshly grated Parmesan cheese*
¼	*pound grated Romano cheese*
1½–2	*cups olive oil*

To make pesto, chop the nuts and garlic, add basil and continue chopping until very fine. Put into a medium bowl and add grated cheeses, salt, and pepper. Slowly pour in olive oil, mixing until creamy.

Place pasta in a large bowl. Toss with 2 cups of the pesto, reserving remainder for another use. Add whole pine nuts and toss well. Blend in additional oil and grated cheese to taste.

Serves 18–20

Lemon Pasta with Salmon

2	*pounds imported pasta*
2	*cups cream*
⅔	*cup lemon juice*
	grated rind of 2 lemons
1	*teaspoon salt*
½	*cup gin or vodka*
12	*ounces cooked fresh salmon*
	pepper to taste

Cook pasta in a large pot of rapidly boiling water. Mix all other ingredients in a medium size bowl. Just before the pasta is cooked al dente remove it from the heat and drain. Return drained pasta to the pot and add remaining mixed ingredients. Cook over medium heat until mixture is absorbed. Serve immediately.

Variation:

~ Add 1–2 cups of cooked vegetables such as peas, zucchini, broccoli spears or carrots.

Serve 8–12

Tagliatelli Primavera

4	*pounds tagliatelli*
3	*carrots, peeled and diced*
10	*fresh asparagus stalks, cut into 1" pieces*
10	*small zucchini, diced*
1	*head cauliflower, broken into florets*
1	*head broccoli, broken into florets*
1	*green pepper, diced*
1	*red pepper, diced*
3	*Jerusalem artichokes, peeled and sliced*
½	*cup olive oil*
½	*cup basil, chopped*
½	*cup parsley*
	Parmesan cheese, grated

Cook pasta until done. Drain, rinse with cold water, and drain again. Cook all the vegetables, except peppers and artichokes, until tender but still crisp. Rinse with cold water and drain.

Toss the pasta with the vegetables. Add oil, basil, parsley, artichokes, and peppers, and sprinkle with grated cheese. Toss again.

Serves 20–24

Italian Sausage Lasagna

2	*tablespoons olive oil*
1	*clove garlic, chopped*
I	*onion, chopped*
1½	*pounds sweet Italian sausage*
3	*cups Marinara sauce*

1   *pound lasagna noodles*
1   *pound Ricotta or cottage cheese*
1   *pound Mozzarella cheese, thinly sliced*
½   *cup grated Parmesan cheese*

Preheat oven to 350°. In a saucepan, sauté garlic in oil for 5 minutes. Remove sausage from casing and add to saucepan. Cook over medium heat until sausage is brown and crumbly; drain excess fat, stir in Marinara sauce.

Cook lasagna noodles until done. Drain, and rinse with cold water while gently separating noodles to prevent them from sticking to each other. Cover a 9 x 13 inch baking dish with a thin layer of sauce, add a layer of noodles, then sauce, ricotta cheese, and mozzarella cheese. Continue layering until pan is filled, ending with sauce. Sprinkle all with Parmesan cheese. Bake 30–35 minutes until bubbly.

Serves 12

If serving lasagna, use packaged ready-to-use dry noodles that don't have to be boiled in water, or purchase your favorite brand of frozen lasagna and bake it in one of your own casserole dishes. No one will notice that you didn't make it from scratch.

Blueberry and Peach Tartlets

Pastry Shells:
½   *pound unsalted butter, softened*
½   *cup sugar*
1   *egg yolk*
1½   *cups flour pinch of salt*

Filling:

2	*cups milk*
1	*egg*
3	*egg yolks*
½	*cup sugar*
6	*tablespoons flour*
½	*teaspoon vanilla*
½	*cup peaches, thinly sliced*
½	*cup blueberries*
2	*tablespoons apricot preserves, strained*

To make pastry shells, cream together butter, sugar, and salt. Add egg yolk, then flour, and mix until smooth. Form into ball, cover, and refrigerate 1 hour. Roll dough out to ¼ inch thickness and cut into 4 inch rounds. Press into 3 inch greased tart pans and refrigerate for 30 minutes.

Preheat oven to 350°. Bake empty tart shells for 10 minutes, until golden brown. Set aside to cool.

To make filling, bring milk to a boil in a saucepan, and allow to cool. Cream the egg, egg yolks, and sugar together. Add in flour, vanilla, and a little of the hot milk to blend. Add the egg mixture to the pan and cook, stirring continuously, until thick and smooth like custard. Remove from heat, cover with wax paper, and let cool.

Fill tart shells half-full with cooled custard. Top filling with peaches and blueberries to cover.

Mix apricot preserves with water, bring to boil, and strain to make 2 tablespoons. Cool and brush over fruit to glaze.   **Makes 12**

11
ORGANIZING THE
BRIDAL SHOWER

*N*OW THAT YOU'VE HAD A CHANCE to explore the wide variety of themes, styles, and types of showers available, it's finally time to decide on size and theme and commit your decisions to writing. The following work sheets will help you organize all your party details, from your menu to the well-stocked bar, and are designed to make the process as painless as possible.

- **Menu and beverage work sheet** — food and drinks are central to your party's success. Planning helps keep you within your budget.

- **Bar checklist** — these items plus a smile will be everything you'll need for a great bar.

- **Party equipment checklist** — all the necessities imaginable to make sure you're ready.

- **Decorating and supplies work sheet** — these are the small and not-so-small touches that will give your shower its flair.

MENU AND BEVERAGE WORK SHEET

Number of Guests ————————————

Type of Shower: ☐ Sit Down   ☐ Buffet   ☐ Breakfast
☐ Brunch   ☐ Luncheon   ☐ Afternoon Tea
☐ Dessert Party   ☐ Cocktails & Hors d'Oeuvres
☐ Dinner

Hors d'Oeuvres: ——————————————————
————————————————————————————————
————————————————————————————————
————————————————————————————————

Salads: ——————————————————————
————————————————————————————————
————————————————————————————————
————————————————————————————————

Main Course: —————————————————————
————————————————————————————————
————————————————————————————————
————————————————————————————————

Other Dishes: ————————————————————
————————————————————————————————
————————————————————————————————
————————————————————————————————

Desserts: —————————————————————
————————————————————————————————
————————————————————————————————
————————————————————————————————

Beverages: ————————————————————
————————————————————————————————
————————————————————————————————
————————————————————————————————

BAR CHECKLIST

Bar Supplies
Ice bucket
Ice tongs
Ice pick
Sharp knife
Corkscrew
Bottle opener
Jigger measures
Large mixing pitcher
Long handled spoon
Shaker/strainer
Blender
Lemon/lime squeezer
Coasters or cocktail napkins

Bar Accompaniments
Ice (½ to ¾ pounds per person)
Lemons, limes, oranges
Green olives
Cocktail onions
Lemon zester
Cocktail toothpicks

Mixers
mineral waters
Club soda
Tonic
Ginger ale
Soft drinks
Orange and tomato juices
Bloody Mary mix

Liquor
Rum: 1 light & 1 dark
Bourbon
Gin
Vodka
Scotch
Blended Whiskey
Dry Vermouth
Sweet Vermouth

Liqueurs
Amaretto
Bailey's Irish Cream
Cognac
Cassis
Cointreau
Dubonnet
Frangelico
Grand Marnier
Kahlua

Beer
Imported beer
Micro-brewery beer
Light and dark beer
Non-alcoholic beer

Wines
White wine
Red wine
Champagne
Wine Coolers
Port
Assorted Sherries

PARTY EQUIPMENT CHECKLIST

Use the following checklist to keep track of all the party equipment you'll need.

Items	Size	Number Needed	Have ✔
Banquet Tables: 4', 6', 8' long			
Round Tables:			
36" diameter seats 4–6			
48" diameter seats 6			
54" diameter seats 8			
60" diameter seats 10			
Misc. Tables			
Folding Chairs			
Umbrellas			
Portable Barbecue			
Lattices			
Heaters			
Tiki Torches			
Lighting			
Banquet Tablecloths			
Circular Tablecloths			
Napkins			

Items	Size	Number Needed	Have ✓
China:			
Dinner Plate			
Luncheon Plate			
Salad Plate			
Cup and Saucer			
Creamer and Sugar			
Serving Platters			
Serving Bowls, 9″			
Wine Glasses			
Champagne Glasses			
Water Goblets			
Cordials, Shot Glasses			
Hi Ball Glasses: 8 oz., 12 oz.			
Water Pitcher			
Salt & Pepper Shaker Set			
Punch Bowl with Ladle			
Glass Serving Bowl, 9″			
4-Tier Serving Tray			
Chafing Dish with Sterno			
Coffee Maker			
Coffee Urn, Stainless or Silver			
Silver Coffee Server			

Items	Size	Number Needed	Have ✓
Silverware:			
Dinner Fork			
Salad Fork			
Dessert Fork			
Dinner Knife			
Spoons			
Serving Fork			
Serving Spoon			
Pastry Trays			
Salad Tongs			
Ice Tongs			
Cake Knife			
Cake or Pie Server			
Silver Tongs			
Bread Baskets			
Bar Buckets			
Bar Towels			
Ice Tub			

DECORATING AND SUPPLIES WORK SHEET

	Type, Color, Size, Amount	✓
Invitations:		
Decorations:		
Balloons		
Baskets		
Streamers, Banners		
Flowers		
Candles		
Other:		
Table Supplies:		
Paper Tablecloth		
Napkins		
Cups		
Plastic Utensils		
Place Cards		
Party Favors		
Other:		
Games:		
Pencils, sharpened		

Paper or Note Pads

Stopwatch or Egg Timer

Items to Play the Game

Party Prizes

Other:

12
BRIDAL SHOWER THEMES

*B*RIDAL SHOWERS are even more fun when they have a theme which determines the type of gifts to bring. If the bride-to-be already has a household of her own, it would be wise to consult with her regarding her preference. Once you have settled on a theme, you can start planning your decorations accordingly. Be sure to include your theme on the invitation itself.

The following themes can be combined with invitations, decorating, and party favor ideas from other chapters. Mix and match your favorites to create a distinctive shower.

A Miscellaneous Shower

True to its name, anything and everything goes with this popular shower! Guests are free to bring whatever they wish in the way of gifts. Despite the increasing popularity of theme showers, the miscellaneous shower is still the most common. It works especially well for the couples party. Although there is no designated gift theme, a decorating theme can still be set. Choose whatever appeals to you, from An Elegant Afternoon Tea to a Tostada Party — any and all food and decorating choices are acceptable. Increase eye appeal by choosing terrific linens, dramatic centerpieces, and interesting party favors. Spending less time on a theme lets you go all out on your decorations!

A Gift Basket Shower

This is one of my favorites! Each guest brings a basket, box, or container filled with imaginative goodies for a designated area of the house. It allows your guests to be creative in their selection of items to get the bride off to a good start. Opening the baskets involves everyone in the fun as they watch the wide variety of goodies selected. You can either tell each guest the theme of her particular basket or leave it to the discretion of the individual. In the latter, it might be helpful to include a list of basket content suggestions to choose from. When they RSVP, they can also tell you which basket they've chosen to bring.

Make this shower an afternoon luncheon by packing individual box lunches consisting of quiche, sandwiches, pasta salads, chips, and giant brownies for dessert. You can also use decorative lap trays and have the guests serve themselves from a buffet table.

Kitchen Basket — Pile a colander or fruit basket with a variety of small kitchen goodies. Look for a grater, mushroom brush, potato peeler, pot holders, and kitchen magnets, all in bright and cheery colors. Incorporate the savory smells of a cucumber hand-wash and soaps scented with vanilla, cinnamon, or orange peel.

Bath Basket — Use a cute wastepaper basket to carry nice soaps, bath salts, loofah sponges, fragrant lotions, and luscious bath oils. Cushion your surprises with unusual washcloths or guest towels.

Wedding Accessories Basket — Help the bride gather the necessary items she will need on her special day. Using a pastel wicker desk tray, choose one or more of the following items to get her started on her accessories: a cake knife and server set, toasting glasses, a special pen and lace-trimmed guest book, a frilly garter, and a dainty handkerchief.

Specialty Food Basket — Spoil the bride-to-be with an assortment of delicious foods. You can center your basket around a particular food. Select a coffee and tea basket, a pasta basket, a sweets basket with cookies and marmalades, or a wine and cheese basket. Give specialty popcorn tucked into a personalized popcorn bowl. Prepare a sumptuous assortment of preserves, jams, and honey snuggled in a wicker basket. Line a breadbasket with a cheery checked hand towel, add a pasta maker and fill with an assortment of special sauces, Italian olive oil, and fine vinegars. Stuff your finest container with an appetizing assortment of imported cheeses, tinned pâtes, caviar, and sardines. Tuck in a variety of unusual crackers and complete with a jar of stuffed olives. The possibilities are endless.

Herb and Spice Basket — Be responsible for the spice in her life by starting your girlfriend off with a tempting selection of herbs and spices. Choose pretty bottles to scatter throughout the basket or place in a spice rack. Tuck in a variety of dried herbs of different hues tied with ribbons

To make your search a breeze, visit our website at www.beverlyclark collection.com or send for a free catalog to:

The Beverly Clark Collection

1120 Mark Avenue

Carpinteria, CA 93013

Tel: 877-862-3933

or pieces of cord. A wreath of herbs adds an artistic touch. If the bride is a gardener, include packets of garden seeds to start her very own herb garden. Herb posters and books can provide much enjoyment.

Picnic Basket — A few guests may want to pitch in for this one. Either assemble your own with colorful ceramic plates and mugs, bamboo flatware, food containers, a vacuum flask, glass tumblers, and cloth napkins, or indulge in one already made up. If you're making up your own, a unique touch might be to add one or more of the following: a butterfly net, instant camera, a bottle of champagne, a map of the local parks, a pair of binoculars, and a picnic blanket.

Candle Basket — Choose different color and size candles, decorator matches, candle sticks, holders, scented candles, outdoor citronella candles, birthday candles, a candle snuffer, luminaire bags, a candle making kit, and so on.

Stationery Basket — Fill a handsome container with elegant paper and envelopes, postcards, note cards, different colored pens, seals, stickers, thank you cards, ribbons, and stamps.

High Tech Basket — Include a mouse pad, post-it notes, music/program CDs, floppy disks, and designer papers.

Travel Basket — Tons of items could make up this unique basket. Ear plugs, Evian spray, miniature flashlight, telephone card, upgrade certificates, neck pillow, foot creams, miniature toiletries, mints, lozenges, tissues, books, maps, collapsible umbrella, fold-up bags, language translation tapes or mini-computer, calculators, and travel appliances are among them.

Hobby Basket — Add this basket to your list if the bride has a favorite hobby such as painting, playing tennis, or gardening.

These are just a few of the many creative and useful baskets you can dream up — have fun thinking of more!

A Kitchen Shower

Every home depends on a well-equipped kitchen to run smoothly. There are a number of can't-do-without items that are fun to both give and receive. Since many couples already have a good start on kitchen essentials, talk to the bride and find out what they already have. Make a list of the essentials they are lacking, as well as gadgets that they particularly want. Enclose your list with each invitation to take some of the guesswork out of gift-giving.

Decorations

Keep your party centered around the kitchen — send out potholder or kitchen towel invitations (See Invitations) and present guests with kitchen magnets for party favors. Think of wearing your favorite apron during the party and giving one to the bride the minute she walks through the door. Set your table in style, using kitchen towels as place mats with coordinating dishcloths as napkins. Create an unusual centerpiece out of small kitchen tools jauntily stuck in a ceramic container. Wooden spoons, a potato masher, an egg beater, a rolling pin, and spatulas are colorful items to be used as part of a centerpiece and then given to the bride.

The perfect motif for an all-female luncheon or dinner, you can decide to lay the buffet out on a kitchen counter or stove. The logical choice for elegant serving containers has to be your best and brightest mixing bowls, pots and pans, canisters, and cookie jars!

Kitchen Gift Goodies

measuring spoons and cups
spatulas
vegetable peeler
rolling pin
muffin tins
tea strainer
meat thermometer
nut grinder
butter cube cutter
lettuce spinner
tea kettle
popcorn popper
waffle iron
juicer
cookbooks
wooden spoons
potato masher
round pie plates
colander
double boiler
roasting pan
garlic press
cake decorating kit
wire whisks
souffle dish
electric hand mixer
electric coffee grinder
electric skillet
wok
bread knife
lemon zester
oven mitt

microwave dishes
rotary egg beater
small vegetable brush
square cake tins
cheese grater
egg poacher
ladle
egg slicer
ice cream scoop
kitchen timer
quiche dish
cappuccino/espresso coffee maker
toaster oven
salad bowl
cookbook holder
manual can opener
set of mixing bowls
cookie sheet
set of cutting knives
omelette pan
butter or sauce brush
cheese slicer
vegetable steamer
melon baller
electric blender
electric coffee maker
electric carving knife
automatic can opener
carving board
non-stick cooking utensils
kitchen shears
pizza stone

A Recipe Shower

A recipe shower is the place for all the cooks to shine as each guest brings his or her favorite recipe affixed to an item or two required in its preparation.

Send each invitation with its own set of instructions and a recipe card to be filled out. Ask each guest to neatly write out the list of ingredients and cooking directions for one of her favorite culinary delights. The gift she chooses should have something to do with the preparation of her favorite recipe. The attached recipe cards will later be placed in a special recipe box purchased by the hostess. Many recipe boxes come already supplied with matching index cards for recipes. Include these or make your own after measuring the recipe box you want to use.

A recipe shower is a nice choice for a brunch or dinner. Use general decorations or rely on the ideas presented in the section on kitchen showers. You can make up menus to use as place mats and give recipe holders as party favors!

Be sure that your gifts match your recipes. Here are a few combinations to get you started:

Hire an outside agency such as "The Pampered Chef" for a kitchen shower. The bride gets to make out her "wish" list and guests buy the items she wants. Check with the local Chamber of Commerce for names of local vendors.

Blueberry Muffins — two muffin tins wrapped in oversized bright napkins.

Quiche — a cheese grater and ceramic quiche dish.

Chocolate Chip Cookies — two cookie sheets holding a bag of chocolate chips, a spatula, and colorful paper napkins.

Belgian Waffles — a Belgian waffle iron and a bottle of pure maple syrup.

Custard Surprise — six custard cups with tiny custard spoons.

Delicious Apple Pie — a ceramic pie plate and a rolling pin.

Double Trouble Chocolate Cake — mixing bowls with a battery-powered flour sifter.

Terrific Lasagna — a baking dish and a manual pasta maker and rack.

A Lingerie Shower

With its lace and frills, this is the perfect shower to have at An Elegant Afternoon Tea. Use fresh flowers for your centerpiece and accent everything with your finest linens, silver, china, and serving pieces. Potpourri sachets for party favors provide a nice touch at each place setting.

For those more adventurous hostesses, try kidnapping the bride for an early morning breakfast surprise or get nostalgic and make it a pajama party!

A lingerie shower is great for the encore bride or the woman who already has a completely stocked kitchen.

Lingerie Gift Ideas

night gowns	teddies
slips	camisoles
lingerie bags	drawer and closet sachets
slippers	laundry bag
robes	bras
lacy underwear	garter belt
stockings	stocking holder
fabric covered hangers	jewelry bags for travel
night shirt	pajamas
kimonos	

A Linen Shower

With great decorator designs to choose from, linens are no longer a boring necessity but have become an exciting part of the bridal trousseau.

Linens can be quite expensive so do keep finances in mind when planning this shower. Many linen showers are just for the bride's relatives who would plan on giving more costly shower gifts anyway. It is also possible to have the bride register for her preferred colors and patterns so that guests may purchase individual parts of a set — one friend can buy the flat sheet, another the pillow cases, and so forth. Another alternative is to have the guests pool their money so that a small group of friends could purchase a tablecloth with another being responsible for matching napkins.

Unless the bride has decided to register for her linens, be sure to specify table and bed sizes, as well as the colors of her prospective kitchen, bath, and bedroom on the invitation. Send out printed invitations or white cloth napkins as a creative alternative. (See Invitations.)

You may choose to make this an afternoon, ladies-only party or a couples evening event, since all the gifts will be for both the bride and groom. Select your favorite style and decorate accordingly.

Gifts for the Linen Closet

tablecloth	place mats
kitchen rug	pillow cases
comforter	duvet cover
mattress pad	dust ruffle and pillow shams
bath, hand, and face towels	bath mat

napkins   silver napkin holders
sheets   blankets
chenille throw   pillow covers
pillows and pillow rolls   night light
beach towels   guest towels
kitchen towels

Time-of-Day Shower

This is a version of the traditional around-the-clock shower which combines the best of two different showers into one — you have the variety of a miscellaneous shower and the fun of having a theme to build your party around.

The guests are each assigned a specific time of day on their invitations. They must then select a gift appropriate for their designated time. In the instructions you include on the invitation, be sure to ask the guests to write the time of day the gift is for on a small gift tag and attach it to the present. This way the bride sees and announces the time of day before opening the gift. Distribute the hours according to the number of guests and the times of day that you think are the most appropriate. Friends may also attach a short note to the gift explaining exactly what they think the bride will be doing at the designated time. These notes are usually funny rather than serious and liven up the gift opening.

Contact a gift basket company in your area to make up individual gift baskets for busy guests to present to the bride.

Make clock invitations to send out (See Invitations) and decorate your party room with clocks and calendars. Use pages from a large desktop calendar as place mats. Pass out fun, inexpensive watches, appointment books, or cute egg timers for party favors.

Timely Gift Suggestions

Morning Hours

newspaper subscription	alarm clock
lit makeup mirror	warming basket for rolls
omelette pan	mugs and mug tree
bathrobe	make-up bag with brushes
breakfast cookbook	waffle iron
coffee maker	electric kettle
thermos coffee mug	electric juicer
yogurt maker	blender
exercise weights	

Midday

appointment book	key finder
address book	wallet
telephone message center	calendar
earrings	scarf
purse	answering machine
calculator	cell phone paraphernalia
umbrella	briefcase
water bottle carrier	CD holder
books on tape	CDs and music tapes

Evening Hours

best-selling books	brandy sniffers
certificate for a massage	pillows
aromatherapy candle	lingerie
a video cassette	monopoly game
cocktail shaker	dessert cookbook
theater tickets	bath oil
classical tapes and CDs	a backgammon board
computer game software	bottle of wine and two glasses

A Honeymoon Shower

The perfect way to say "bon voyage' to the happy couple — this prenuptial party will supply them with a variety of travel accessories for their wedding trip. A honeymoon shower may be the ideal choice for a couples gathering or a fantastic way to salute the encore bride. Plan a buffet with the couples honeymoon destination in mind, featuring a culinary delight from that region of the world. Let your decorations show how the couple will be traveling, as well as their destination. Centerpieces can cheerfully contain toy trains, miniature cars, plastic boats, and cardboard busses. A trip to the local nature store or travel store will provide great ideas and items. Turn to travel posters, maps, and world globes to set the mood of your party. If the couple is bound for Hawaii, don't forget to scatter a lei or two around the room. You may want to finish off your decorating by playing the type of music popular where they will be going.

Gift certificate shower where guests provide gift certificates to the bride's favorite stores saves everyone time.

No matter where they're headed or how they are getting there, thoughtful gifts will always come in handy.

Just-the-ticket Gifts

travel alarm clock	rolls of film
photo album	travel iron
travel shaving kit	shoe bags
laundry kit with line and clips	first aid kit
miniature flashlight	ear plugs
travel pillow	beach towels
hanging garment bag	travel hair dryer
guidebooks	travel diary
luggage cart on wheels	plastic-lined makeup bag

jewelry roll
nail kit
self-tanning lotion
travel games
travel electric curlers
money roll or belt
foreign language phrase book
foreign current converter and adapter
small amount of foreign currency traveler's checks

lingerie bag
sun screen
sun hat
carry-on luggage
leather passport case
pocket calculator

An Entertaining Shower

As its title says, this one is geared toward the bride who has already collected the basics and is now looking forward to entertaining in her new home.

Definitely designed for couples, the entertaining shower is perfect for a Sunday brunch, an exciting cocktail party, or an elegant dinner affair. They all create the ideal setting to shower the new couple with those special gifts guaranteed to make entertaining a breeze.

It's not necessary to have a particular decorating theme since the party itself is the theme — entertaining and doing it in style is the feeling of this one.

A group of friends may want to join forces and purchase a punch bowl set or an elegant chafing dish to get the couple off to a good start.

Other Entertaining Thoughts

cheese board and slicer
electric warming tray
bar glasses
cloth cocktail napkins
crystal stemware

chips and dip set
nut and candy dishes
champagne glasses
lace tablecloth
wine decanter

crystal water pitcher
cocktail forks and knives
wine opener
indoor hibachi
hors d-oeuvres tray
popcorn popper
ice bucket with tongs
martini pitcher
Trivial Pursuit game
his and hers aprons

cocktail shaker and jigger
wine rack
barbecue utensils
relish dish
fondue pot
serving trays
bottle opener
silver-plated coasters
videos

An Around-the-World Shower

This type of shower affords an international flavor with many exotic gifts. Each guest is assigned a country and then purchases a gift with that country in mind. For example, China might buy a set of chopsticks with rice bowls, a bamboo steamer, or a teapot with a supply of ginseng tea. Italy might buy a pasta maker, espresso coffee pot, or an Italian cookbook. How about an Irish wool throw or a colorful silk sarong from Bali? Guests can feast upon worldly fare. The possibilities are endless.

More Imaginative Ideas:

Portugal — Pottery, lace linens
Nigeria — Woven baskets, wooden serving utensils
Mexico — Tortilla warmer, garden statuary
Japan — Sushi kit, sake set
France — Soup tureen, truffles
England — Bone china teacups, garden basket

13
OPENING THE GIFTS AND FAVORS

Opening the Gifts

*F*OR GIFT OPENING with a twist, have a secretly selected secretary write down exactly what the bride says when she opens each gift. After all the presents have been opened, read the quotes out loud.

Be sure to designate the helpers — you need someone to keep track of the gifts and who they were given by. Also, someone can be appointed to make a bouquet out of the ribbons and bows from all the packages. For a simple yet fun bouquet, use a paper plate with an X cut in the center. Draw the ribbons through the slit, gathering the bows into a colorful bunch on the plate. Add your stick-on bows around the center grouping to cover the entire plate, making the brides first bouquet! Later, this fun bouquet can be the traditional stand-in flowers at the wedding rehearsal.

As hostess of the bridal shower, you may wish to offer a special gift of pre-addressed note cards and envelopes for each guest, complete with a stamp. Give these to the bride along with the checklist of gifts. This is a great help for the busy weeks before the wedding.

If you prefer a ready-made base for the ribbon bouquet check Beverly Clark's website at beverlyclarkcollection.com for the heart shaped Ribbon Bow-K ™!

More and more people use a camcorder to record each event. Make sure you have one guest who can provide this, or if your budget allows ask a professional to attend for all or part of the gathering. If the bride and groom are hiring a videographer for their wedding and have a video package, let them know ahead of time as they may wish to have the shower included. This will be part of the video shared at the wedding reception.

Why Favors?

Favors serve as decorations and as token thank-you gifts for the guests who make time to celebrate and contribute to the future home of the bride and groom. Putting in the extra effort to provide favors makes all the difference, whether they are home-made or purchased. Simple things like attaching a cookie cutter to a card can look just as impressive as pretty silver frames, so consider your time and budget requirements. Short of ideas? Check your local magazine stand where you'll find lots of clever motifs.

Try wrapping your favors up in interesting packets. Consider fabric and cellophane bags. Look for colorful and inexpensive lunch bags or use shiny, iridescent cellophane, art papers, or some of the designer wrapping paper available.

Favors with Flair

Potpourri sachet — Available in a wide variety of shapes, sizes, and fabrics, prices are as varied as the selection! You can make your own by cutting 5 inch squares of fine netting, lace, or fabric or using a handmade handkerchief and placing a few tablespoons of scented potpourri in the center. Gather the edges and secure with a matching ribbon. These are great for a An Elegant Afternoon Tea or lingerie shower.

Chocolate long-stemmed rose — Tie a gold filigree bow around each one, add a card with the name of the guest and voila! You've just created a place card, too. Or arrange a stunning centerpiece and instruct your guests to each take a rose as they leave. You can make your own.

Chocolate heart or swan — Fill heart-shaped shells or the empty niches in the swans' backs with Jordan almonds or chocolate truffles and then wrap in colored cellophane. Find these delights at specialty chocolate stores.

Chocolate truffles — Many chocolate manufacturers sell small individual boxes containing one or two truffles. Decorate the boxes with a ribbon or use your own boxes or wrapping.

Chocolate mints — Exclusive chocolate stores carry individually wrapped chocolate mints tied in sets of three. Make your own for less money by purchasing an entire box of mints, dividing and wrapping up in cellophane.

Chocolate-dipped spoons — Again, you can find these in gift, kitchen, coffee and chocolate specialty stores. You can also make your own.

Chocolate Dipped Spoons

1   *16 ounce block melting chocolate of your choice*
     cellophane wrap
     wax paper
     ribbon
     party plastic spoons

Melt chocolate over low heat. Dip spoon in chocolate covering the spoon bowl to just below the handle. Lay flat on wax paper to harden. When ready, wrap with cellophane, and secure in place by tying a small bow.

Yields approximately 36 spoons

A split of champagne — Wrapped in a shiny swatch of fabric or an elegant napkin and adorned with a silver bow, this serves as the most sophisticated of place cards for the formal, sitdown dinner.

Crystal ring holder — Tie a satin ribbon around the center or fill the base with sugared almonds and wrap in cellophane.

Silver dish — Nestle three truffles in a dish, wrap, and top off with an oversized bow.

*

Picture frame — Select delicate picture frames to grace each place setting. Write the guest's name on a piece of paper and place it in the window of each frame. A charming place card, it's something everyone can use.

*

Engraved wine glass — Purchase inexpensive wine glasses and have each one engraved with your guests' names. For a an extra-special effect, tie a helium balloon to the stem and place around the table for each visitor to find.

Porcelain or crystal bells — Bells are a delicate touch for the elegant table. If you want to go all out, a guest's name can be painted or etched on each bell.

*

Porcelain or fabric-covered boxes — Containers make a favorite container to remind everyone of your special shower.

*

Note paper or thank-you cards — These may be personalized with each guest's initials so that they can also serve as place cards. A pleasing memento, no one can ever have enough!

Bath soaps — Fill a small basket with these scented delights. For two more lavish favors, add fragrant body mousse, bath salts, or a luxurious bath oil.

Gift boxes and baskets — Can be filled with candy, sugared almonds and small items such as miniature soaps or shells.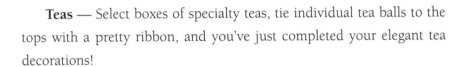

     *   *

Teas — Select boxes of specialty teas, tie individual tea balls to the tops with a pretty ribbon, and you've just completed your elegant tea decorations!

Refrigerator magnet — Perky and fun, an ideal choice for a kitchen shower.

 Small votive candle holders — Use metallic pens to write guest's names. A great favor that doubles for a place card.

Christmas ornament — Just the right touch if Christmas is just around the corner.

Makeup or lipstick brush — A decorative bow adds a whimsical note to this party favor.

Novelty pens — Find fun ballpoint pens in gift and discount stores or make your own with silk flowers and florist's tape.

* Available from *The Beverly Clark Collection*

14
BRIDAL SHOWER GAMES & ENTERTAINMENT

SHOWER ENTERTAINMENT usually centers around socializing, games, and opening the gifts. Depending on your guests, the formality of your party, and your own preferences, you may decide to eliminate the games or relegate them to a relatively minor role in the festivities. To fill the gap, think of hiring a magician, palm reader, or psychic to entertain those special guests. For a couples event, you might want to think in terms of a stand-up comedian or juggler to add pizzazz to your party.

Music

An essential ingredient in creating and sustaining a comfortable mood, music must suit the occasion. Think in terms of soft background music supplied by tapes or records. A low volume guarantees that your guests will have a comfortable background for conversation yet won't have to strain to be heard. A special theme begs for special music. Choose a mariachi band to liven up a tostada party or a pair of strolling fiddlers for an Italian pasta fling. Consider where the bride and groom are headed for their honeymoon. Add music from this country, such as drumming, steel bands, Irish songs, and so forth.

In keeping with the more sophisticated air of the cocktail party or formal dinner, engage a flutist, pianist, or guitarist for entertainment and forego the games. If you want couples to dance, think of renting a jukebox, hiring a disc jockey, or featuring a local band. Music academies, high schools, and community colleges are all excellent sources of good musicians willing to work at reasonable rates. You can also browse through the classified ads of local newspapers and magazines. Don't forget to check the most reliable source you have — your friends.

Games

Bridal Gown Designer

This one calls for some imagination, so let's see how creative your guests can be! Divide the group into two or three teams and place each in a separate room. Supply each of the three teams with several rolls of toilet paper. The teams select their own "bride" and prepare to design an original gown for her out of the toilet paper they have. No tape or pins are allowed. Give your designers about 15–20 minutes to complete their creations and then have everyone except the team brides reassemble in the living room. Call out each team's entry to model for the real bride.

She has the honor of choosing the winning team which has fashioned the most creative dress. Each member of the winning team receives a small prize for her efforts.

High Roller

This is a lively game suitable for any size group. Arrange the guests' chairs in a circle, piling an assortment of wrapped gifts in the center on the floor. Buy one gift for every four to five guests and wrap enticingly. Make each one appear completely different from all the others. Select small items, such as a powder puff or makeup brush, to go into the largest, most expensive looking boxes while you place nicer gifts in "plain Jane" wrappings. Try to pick out prizes that vary widely in size, length, weight, or width. Use two sets of dice (or three, if there are more than 20 players) and pick two players sitting across from each other to start the game. Each gets one roll. If the person rolls doubles, a gift from the center can be selected. When all the gifts have been taken from the center, doubles allows the gambler to pluck a package off someone's lap — this is where the fun really begins! After one roll, the dice are passed to the left. Set the timer for seven minutes and when it goes off, whoever has a present gets to keep it.

Be sure that the winners unwrap their gifts while still seated in the circle — everyone will be surprised at the real contents of each gift! Most often it turns out that the gift everyone seemed to be fighting over is really the silliest present of the bunch! A good game for couples parties, take care to ensure that the items you select are appropriate for both genders.

Tell Me Who I Am?

A perfect starter activity, this game is a great way to get your guests to mingle. Prepare ahead of time by writing the name of a famous person, celebrity, singer, or author on a 3 x 5 inch index card. As each guest arrives, pin one of the secret identities on her back without divulging the name on the card. The task is for the guests to find out exactly who they are by asking others questions which can only be answered with a "yes" or "no." Everyone will begin to mingle in an effort to discover their own identity! The first one to figure out correctly who they are wins. If you've got a super sleuth at the party who guesses correctly almost right away, you may want to continue the game and award second and third prizes.

Clothespin Game

Your guests will enjoy having this one pinned on them! As party guests arrive, clip a clothespin somewhere on their clothes and instruct them that crossing their legs is not allowed for the entire party. If one guest catches another crossing her legs, that person gets to take the guilty party's clothespin and add it to her own collection. If a person transgresses while wearing several clothespins she has captured from other guests, she loses them all. The person with the most pins at the end of the party is declared the winner.

Fill in the Blanks

Each guest receives a pencil and a piece of paper. The sheet contains the word "bridal" written vertically down the left margin with the word "shower" directly across from it on the right side. The object of the game is to use each pair of letters as the beginning and end of the longest word you can think of. The first word, for example, must begin with "b" and end with "s." Numerous possibilities include words such as "brides" or "bouquets." Each letter in the newly created word is worth one point, unless the word pertains directly to a wedding or shower, in which case each letter brings two points. Give everyone ten minutes to rack their brains for words. The one with the most points wins.

The Newlywed Game

Based on the television show, "The Newlywed Game," this party time favorite works well for either a couples or all-women party. The game will take a little more preparation on your part but the results are worth it! Call the groom ahead of time and quiz him about himself and his relationship with his intended. Be sure that whatever you ask him remains a secret so that the bride doesn't know anything ahead of time. List all of your questions on 3 x 5 inch cards and write the groom's answers on the back of each. Here are a few questions to start you out:

"Where did you go on your first date?"

"What did she wear the first time you saw her?"

"What was your last fight about?"

"What's your favorite dish that she cooks?"

"Which habit of hers annoys you the most?"

Make sure that you have asked enough questions so that each person attending the party will have something to ask the bride. To start the game, distribute one card to each guest and have the bride or couple sit in front of the group. Each person then reads the question from her individual card. The bride is not allowed to answer yet but has to wait until all the questions are read. After everyone has had a chance to hear all the questions that will be asked of the bride, have them guess the number of questions that they think the bride will be able to answer correctly, and have them write down their estimates in a corner of their index card. Now the bride can begin to answer the questions one at a time. Each guest reads her question, waits for the brides answer, and then reads the groom's response written on the back of the card. After the bride has given all her answers, tally up her correct responses to see how well she knows her husband-to-be. A prize goes to the guest who comes closest to estimating the number of correct answers.

Take My Advice

Since we all think that we give the best advice, everyone should enjoy this game which gives your guests a chance to really shine as marriage experts. Preprint sheets with a list of 12 "hot" topics on which the guests are to give their advice. Each sentence must start with the word already there ("never" or "always") and should be the guest's own "little gem of wisdom." Feel free to add any other areas of domestic life where you feel the bride might like a few tips. The funnier the advice, the better. The first contestant to finish wins, and gets to share all her advice with the group.

1. (Fighting) Always
2. (Cooking) Never
3. (Laundry) Always
4. (Cleaning) Never
5. (Shopping) Always
6. (Kissing) Never
7. (Fighting) Always
8. (Old Boyfriends) Never
9. (Money) Always

10. (Work) Never
11. (Honesty) Always
12. (In-Laws) Never
13. (E-mail) Never
14. (Travel) Always
15. (Television) Never
16. (Pets) Always

Who Has the Kitchen Sink?

This is a true scavenger hunt in purses. Tell your guests to dig deep in their purses to find as many of the listed items as possible. Items cannot be counted twice, no matter how many of them you actually have. For example, whether your hand bag contains one or five stamps, you still win five points. Ten to fifteen minutes should be ample time for your company to have successfully struggled through the contents of their handbags and resurfaced with ample points. The scavenger with the most points (and messiest bag!) wins.

Postage Stamp	5 pts.	Aspirin	10 pts.
Pencil	5 pts.	Pen	2 pts.
Lipstick	5 pts.	Hand Lotion	10 pts.
Nail Polish	25 pts.	Business Card	10 pts.
Rubber Band	10 pts.	Flashlight	10 pts.
Tweezers	10 pts.	Floppy Disk	25 pts.
Breath Mints	15 pts.	Toothbrush	25 pts.
Chewing Gum	5 pts.	Pen	3 pts.
Pocket Knife	5 pts.	Address Book	15 pts.
Tissues	25 pts.	Nail File	15 pts.
Hair Brush	3 pts.	CDs	10 pts.
Mirror	5 pts.	Eye Glasses	10 pts.
Children Photos	5 pts.	Library Card	15 pts.

Credit Card	5 pts.	Tape Recorder	50 pts.
Sun Block	10 pts.	Map	10 pts.
Cellular Telephone	20 pts.	Whistle	30 pts.
Book	25 pts.	Tea Bag	20 pts.

Wedding Scramble

Find out just how your guests would go about organizing a wedding by having them unscramble the following list of necessary wedding "ingredients:' All the tangled names are things and people commonly found at both ceremony and reception. The first person finished wins. If no one finishes in 10 minutes, award the prize to the person with the most correct answers.

1.	MORGO	2.	GRIN
3.	LDCNAE	4.	RESHUS
5.	TAREGR	6.	SMIEDSIBRAD
7.	STIGF	8.	WORFSEL
9.	KACE	10.	TENBAMS
11.	REBID	12.	LSATEP

The Correct Answers to Wedding Scramble

1.	GROOM	2.	RING
3.	CANDLE	4.	USHERS
5.	GARTER	6.	BRIDESMAIDS
7.	GIFTS	8.	FLOWERS
9.	CAKE	10.	BEST MAN
11.	BRIDE	12.	PETALS

Complete the Sentence

Each guest will receive a printed sheet of paper containing sentences that need to be completed. Allot only five minutes for this one. The contestant with the greatest number of correctly completed sentences wins!

1. A woman's work . . .
2. A happy house . . .
3. Behind every great man . . .
4. A woman's place . . .
5. When the going gets tough . . .
6. A stitch in time . . .
7. My house is . . .
8. The path of true love . . .
9. Variety is . . .
10. Every man's home . . .
11. True love . . .
12. Marriages are . . .
13. A watched pot . . .
14. If the shoe fits . . .
15. A penny saved . . .
16. Home is . . .
17. Too many cooks . . .

Answers to Sentence Completion

1. is never done.
2. is full of laughter.
3. is a successful woman.
4. is in the home.
5. the tough get going (or the wife goes shopping!)
6. saves nine.
7. your house.
8. never runs smooth.
9. the spice of life.
10. is his castle.
11. conquers all.
12. made in heaven.
13. never boils.
14. wear it.

15. is a penny earned.
16. where the heart is.
17. spoil the broth.

In the Dark!

A fun dress up game for the bride. Prepare a small travel bag, with a variety of articles of clothing such as a sun hat, a thong, garden gloves, boxer shorts, a bra, sunglasses, anything else funny, etc. Tell the bride that she is at her honeymoon location but there is no power and she must dress in the dark. Blindfold her and tell her that she must put on all the things in the bag (over her clothes). Be ready with the camera and the camcorder!

Shapes

Use 10–15 plastic grocery bags, (double them if they are thin and see through). Number each with a permanent marker. Place a different household item in each bag and tie the handle ends down so that you cannot see inside and the item will not fall out, as guests will be passing them around. With a timer, allow each guest 15–20 seconds to hold the bag and write down what is inside. After everyone has marked down their assumptions, open them up and share. The person with the most correct guesses wins!!

Prize-Winning Ideas

Be sure that you have stocked up on plenty of prizes. Have one for each game plus a few in reserve in case of ties. When planning a couples shower, make sure that the prizes are appropriate for either a woman or a man.

specialty chocolate	pound of specialty coffee beans
corkscrew	potpourri and drawer sachets
ring dishes	bath salts
jams and jellies	gift certificate for a car wash
CDs	two movie passes
memo pads	coffee mugs
bottle of wine	flavored popcorn in a tin
scarves	special soaps
inspirational books	telephone charge cards

In Closing

Perhaps you are a hostess looking to capture the romance and elegance of this time-honored affair for your best friend. Maybe you've chosen to keep it a simple gathering, adding your personal flair! Whatever spirit you wish to capture, all of the arrangements for a perfect bridal shower are at your fingertips. Hopefully, with the help of this book, you've chosen a location and an exciting theme, selected a menu, and thought up some unique favors for your guests. Now you're ready to entertain and pamper the bride-to-be (and possibly the groom!) and her friends in style. Congratulations on an event everyone will treasure in the years to come.

Resources

Other Beverly Clark books from Wilshire Publications

Weddings: A Celebration by Beverly Clark

Planning a Wedding to Remember (English and Spanish versions) by Beverly Clark

Weddings: A Family Affair by Marjorie Engel

All About Him and All About Her (Romantic guidebooks to be filled out by each partner)

A Special Day for You! (A coloring activity book for children)

To obtain these books, visit your local bookstore or order from your favorite on-line bookseller.

From the Beverly Clark Collection
Bridal accessories with distinction
www.beverlyclark.com or call 877-862-3933 for your closest supplier

From Beverly Clark Enterprises
Finding the wedding and honeymoon locations of your dreams is just a click away!
www.weddinglocation.com and www.beverlyclarktravel.com

About Beverly Clark
Beverly Clark is the best-selling author of *Planning a Wedding to Remember*. She is nationally renowned for her appearances on TV and radio, and in newspapers and magazines. She is also the designer of "The Beverly Clark Collection," a fine line of bridal accessories.

INDEX